THE LIVING GOD AND OUR LIVING PSYCHE

The Living God and Our Living Psyche

What Christians Can Learn from Carl Jung

Ann Belford Ulanov

&

Alvin Dueck

William B. Eerdmans Publishing Company

Grand Rapids, Michigan / Cambridge, U.K.

Published 2008 by

Wm. B. Eerdmans Publishing Co.

2140 Oak Industrial Drive N.E., Grand Rapids, Michigan 49505 /

P.O. Box 163, Cambridge CB3 9PU U.K.

Library of Congress Cataloging-in-Publication Data

Ulanov, Ann Belford.

The living God and our living psyche: what Christians can learn from Carl Jung /

Ann Belford Ulanov & Alvin Dueck.

p.   cm.

Includes bibliographical references.

ISBN 978-0-8028-2467-7 (pbk.: alk. paper)

1. Christianity — Psychology.   2. Jung, C. G. (Carl Gustav), 1875-1961.

3. Psychoanalysis and religion.   I. Dueck, Alvin C., 1943-   II. Title.

BR110.U425   2008

261.5'15 — dc22

2007043608

www.eerdmans.com

For Katy and Michael Blank

my second parents

A.B.U.

Contents

Prologue

On Reading Jung:
Pastoring the Modern Psyche

Why should Christians read Jung? Why bother with a psychologist/psychiatrist deceased for more than forty years, who wrote in a European context and whose approach is used by a minority of mental-health practitioners? There are those, Christians included, who reject Jung as politically naïve, individualistic, psychologically reductionistic, morally ambiguous, elitist, and Gnostic.[1] His view of women has been dismissed as essentialist and stereotyped.[2] In some circles, his psychology is relegated to the occult or disparaged as New Age.[3] Another problem for many is Jung's strange lan-

1. Andrew Samuels, *Jung and the Post-Jungians* (London: Routledge & Kegan Paul, 1985); and Jeffrey Satinover, *The Empty Self: C. G. Jung and the Gnostic Foundations of Modern Identity* (Westport, Conn.: Hamewith Books, 1996).

2. For varying perspectives, see Naomi R. Goldenberg, *Important Directions for a Feminist Critique of Religion in the Works of Sigmund Freud and Carl Jung* (New Haven, Conn.: Yale, 1976); S. Rowland, *Jung: A Feminist Revision* (Malden, Mass.: Polity, 2002); and Demaris S. Wehr, *Jung and Feminism: Liberating Archetypes* (Boston: Beacon Press, 1989).

3. Richard Noll likens Jung to David Koresh and Jim Jones. He describes analytical psychology as a "Swiss cult of middle-class, sun-worshipping neopagans led by a charismatic man who experienced himself to be Christ." See Richard Noll, "The Rose, the Cross,

We gratefully acknowledge comments made on the prologue and epilogue by Ann Belford Ulanov, Deborah van Deusen Hunsinger, David Augsburger, David Atkins, and Richard Peace. We thank Kathryn Streeter, Barbara Bell, and Daniel Groot for assistance in copyediting.

guage of the collective unconscious, synchronicity, and alchemy. His theory, some argue, is a rival religion that assumes an unfallen human nature, so mired in the morass of subjectivism that the life, death, and resurrection of Christ have no objective meaning.[4] Phillip Rieff concluded, "Better an outright enemy [Freud] than an untrustworthy friend [Jung]."[5]

In the middle of the last century, the antipathy of evangelical Christians toward psychology generally and toward Jung in particular was rooted, in part, in the reaction of nineteenth-century Protestantism to the rise of modernity. For conservative Christians, psychology was a heresy propagated by modern culture.[6] Jung's work, like Freud's work, constituted not a return to faith, but rather a manifestation of an agnostic liberalism.[7] Spirituality should be biblically rooted, and matters of the soul were the province of theology, not psychology. For them, Jung had too low a view of the authority of Christian Scriptures and doctrine and hence was viewed as extremely relativistic.

One wonders: Can good come out of Zurich? Novelists seem to think

---

and the Analyst," *New York Times,* 15 October 1994. For a more careful analysis, see Sonu Shamdasani, *Cult Fictions: C. G. Jung and the Founding of Analytical Psychology* (New York: Routledge, 1998), and also *Jung and the Making of Modern Psychology: The Dream of a Science* (New York: Cambridge University Press, 2003).

4. Paul C. Vitz, "Secular Personality Theories: A Critical Analysis," in *Man and Mind: A Christian Theory of Personality,* ed. T. Burke (Hillsdale, Mich.: Hillsdale College Press, 1987), pp. 65-94; Roger Hurding, *Roots and Shoots* (London: Hodder & Stoughton, 1985), pp. 334-60; and Alasdair MacIntyre, "Jung, Carl Gustav," in *The Encyclopedia of Philosophy,* vols. 3-4, ed. P. Edwards (New York: Macmillan, 1967), pp. 294-96. Stan Jones and Richard Butman conclude their review of Jung as follows: "The experiential nature of analytic psychology resists an external, authoritative understanding of truth, emphasizing, in contrast, the personal myth and story of the individual. Thus the Christian reader of Jung and Jungian psychology must be extremely cautious when encountering phrases and concepts borrowed from Christian theology." See Stan Jones and Richard Butman, *Modern Psychotherapies: A Comprehensive Christian Appraisal* (Downers Grove, Ill.: InterVarsity Press, 1991), p. 122.

5. Rieff, *The Triumph of the Therapeutic: Uses of Faith after Freud* (New York: Harper & Row, 1966), p. 91.

6. Martin Bobgan and Deidre Bobgan, *Psycho Heresy: The Psychological Seduction of Christianity* (Santa Barbara, Calif.: EastGate Publishers, 1987).

7. T. G. Esau, "The Evangelical Christian in Psychotherapy," *American Journal of Psychotherapy* 52 (1998): 28-36.

so. Canadian writer Robertson Davies and British novelist Susan Howatch[8] have borrowed heavily from Jung. For Howatch, that borrowing was for the sake of a deeper spirituality. Ann Belford Ulanov, arguably America's foremost theological interpreter of Jung, finds much in his work that is spiritually and psychologically helpful, and her essays on Jung and Christianity are featured in this book.[9]

The focus of this book is a conversation between Jung and Christianity, a dialogue that we believe will yield insights for pastors, psychologists, and Christians generally. We propose in this prologue that Carl Gustav Jung, the son of a Reformed minister, wrote a *pastoral* response to the rise of secularism and the decline of religiosity in his day. His was an attempt to rescue religion from the tentacles of modern skepticism. In the soul of the secular modern, he was able to discern a spiritual presence that, he hoped, could sustain the individual through the vicissitudes of modernity. Rising through the last several centuries, modernity had reached the apex of its power in the first half of the twentieth century, and its capitulation to science had drained away much of the healing power of Christian practices. Jung sought to recover this vitality.

While there are aspects of Jung's approach with which we differ (the subject addressed in the epilogue), we believe Jung has a contribution to make to the Christian community. This prologue will provide a context by reviewing the ways in which Jung's anthropology was a *pastoral* response to counter the corrosive effects of modernity on the psyche. We conclude this prologue by introducing the reader to Ann Belford Ulanov and her essays.

8. See Davies, *The Cornish Trilogy* (New York: Viking, 1991); *The Salterton Trilogy* (New York: Penguin Books, 1991); and *The Deptford Trilogy* (New York: Penguin Books, 1990). And see Howatch, *Glamorous Powers* (New York: A. A. Knopf, 1988); *Glittering Images* (New York: Ballantine Books, 1988); *Mystical Paths* (New York: HarperCollins, 1992); *Scandalous Risks* (New York: A. A. Knopf, 1990); *Ultimate Prizes* (New York: Random House, 1989); *Absolute Truths* (London: HarperCollins, 1994); *The Wonder-Worker: A Novel* (New York: Random House, 1997); and *The High Flyer* (Rockland, Mass.: Wheeler Pub., 1999).

9. These essays were originally lectures that Ulanov delivered at Fuller Theological Seminary's School of Psychology during the Integration Symposium, February 18-20, 2004. We are grateful to Evelyn and Frank Freed, whose endowment to the Graduate School of Psychology made the symposium possible.

Jung, Religion, and Modernity

We submit that Jung is best understood in the context of the complex web of interrelationships between modernity, religion, and psychology. Neither psychology as a discipline nor religion in individuals and institutions functions in a social vacuum. Both have been profoundly shaped by a search in the past half-millennium for self-evident truths to replace the arbitrary authority of monarchs or divine revelation. In contrast to feudalism and medievalism, modernity highlighted the significance of individual freedom, uniqueness, worth, sufficiency, and creativity.[10] It elevated the role of an ahistorical, acontextual, propositional rationality in order to create societal coherence and avoid a repetition of the debacle of the religious wars of 1618 to 1648.[11] Modernity articulated a linear, instrumental reason for the emerging industrial society, while Romanticism reacted to industrialization by sacralizing experience. With the rise of science, religion was relegated to the realm of private preference at best, and superstition at worst. The discovery of universal truth as the revealed order in nature replaced older sacred texts, and the significance of *logos* was made dependent on its ability to link thought to objective reality.[12]

In this context, modern psychology emerged. Peter Homans has pointed out that conditions were ripe for the development of psychology as a discipline, since there was a decline in the power of tradition to shape personal life, an emergence of heightened personal self-consciousness, a split in personal self-consciousness from the social order, and a devaluation of the societal.[13] Furthermore, since empirical science was the privileged epistemology in modernity, the discipline of psychology, in order to be legitimated, adopted scientific procedures for gaining knowledge.

10. Steven Lukes, *Individualism* (Oxford: Basil Blackwell, 1984).

11. Stephen Toulmin, *Cosmopolis: The Hidden Agenda of Modernity* (Chicago: University of Chicago Press, 1993).

12. Alvin Dueck and Thomas D. Parsons, "Integration Discourse: Modern and Postmodern," *Journal of Psychology and Theology* 32 (2004): 232-47.

13. Homans, *Jung in Context: Modernity and the Making of a Psychology* (Chicago: University of Chicago Press, 1995). See also Charles Taylor, *Sources of the Self: The Making of the Modern Identity* (Cambridge: Cambridge University Press, 1989).

That which was not observable (e.g., experience, religious sensibilities) was excluded in favor of the study of concrete, specific behaviors. The knowledge that emerged was presumed to be universal. With the rise of capitalist bureaucracy, the need to make decisions about the abilities of the workforce encouraged the development of the testing industry.[14] Psychology now fit the modern ethos.

At the turn of the twentieth century, the new field of the psychology of religion began to apply general findings and broad psychological theories to the experience of religion. Although William James thought that intense religious experiences were worthy of psychological attention,[15] subsequent psychologists saw the religious person as one who persisted in an illusion, who used religion as a coping mechanism, or worse, as one who could simply be understood as a result of internal psychological and external cultural forces. It should come as no surprise, given this analysis, that the conversation between religionists and psychologists over the past century has been faltering.[16]

Theologians and lay Christians today are no more immune to the hegemony of modernity than were those engaged early in the discipline of psychology. What began as "warfare" between science and religion has, over the centuries, become a partnership, with occasional flare-ups over creationism and the role of free will. However, faith has been rendered largely an individual and private experience, with more concern to actualize innate personal potential than to advocate publicly for social jus-

---

14. Philip Cushman, *Constructing the Self, Constructing America: A Cultural History of Psychotherapy* (Boston: Addison-Wesley, 1995).

15. James, *The Varieties of Religious Experience: A Study in Human Nature* (New York: Modern Library, 1902/1999).

16. Alvin Dueck and Thomas Parsons, "Ethics, Alterity, and Psychotherapy: A Levinasian Perspective," *Pastoral Psychology* 55 (2007): 271-82. See the introduction in this article for a review of psychology of religion as a modern enterprise. Also relevant is James Carrette, "The Challenge of Critical Psychology," in *Religion and Psychology: Mapping the Terrain: Contemporary Dialogues, Future Prospects,* ed. Diane Jonte-Pace and William B. Parson (New York: Routledge, 2001), pp. 110-26; and Keith Meador, "My Own Salvation," in *The Secular Revolution: Power, Interests, and Conflict in the Secularization of American Public Life,* ed. Christian Smith (Berkeley and Los Angeles: University of California Press, 2003), pp. 269-309.

tice or environmental protection. Morality has been reduced to ethical rules that are presumed to be universally applicable.[17] There are even those religionists who have seen modernity as a new and positive cultural movement to which the church and its adherents should adapt.

Jung's Pastoral Response

While some might say that Jung capitulated to modernism, we suggest that he engaged in a *pastoral* attempt to counter the personally debilitating effects of modernity.[18] Given Jung's highly secularized European context, he wondered, in his work with clients who espoused no interest in religious matters, how one could address issues of spirituality without sounding moralistic, didactic, or sermonic.[19] Jung suggested that psychologists look for evidence of the transcendent in the unconscious experiences of their clients. Like a pastor, Jung reflected on the psychological condition of the modern individual from a cultural perspective, and also on the state of European civilization with a concern for its healing. Since the modern psyche proved unable to contain mystery, ambiguity, and contradiction, Jung not only elucidated these psychological states in therapy but also incorporated them in his theory of the person. He countered the modern tendency to split the individual from culture, the rational from the irrational. Unlike many moderns, Jung actually valued past wisdom and non-Western ways of thinking. Jung, *qua* pastor, was hopeful.

Jung responded prophetically to the hubris of Enlightenment foundationalism and its obsession with certitude.[20] He did not subscribe

17. John Rawls, *A Theory of Justice* (Cambridge, Mass.: Belknap Press of Harvard University Press, 1971).

18. In the epilogue following Ulanov's three essays, we will examine some of the ways in which Jung was, in our estimation, less than successful in his counterproposals.

19. See Winston Gooden, "Spiritual Themes in Psychotherapy," in *Integrating Psychology and Theology: Reflections and Research,* ed. Alvin Dueck (Pasadena, Calif.: Fuller Seminary Press, 2006), pp. 113-33.

20. Christopher Hauke, *Jung and the Postmodern: The Interpretation of Realities* (London: Routledge, 2000).

to a simplistic representational epistemology, but proposed that the experience of a stimulus is always more than what the stimulus presents. His was not a theory that connected signs with reality but one that struggled with the complexity and power of the symbolic. Jung's epistemology was not positivist, but diverse enough to include narrative, dreams, fantasy, propositional truth, and ethical pronouncements.

Given this array of responses to modernity, we will focus on three pastoral ways in which Jung addressed the issues of his day. He emphasized the *religious* in contrast to the secular psyche, the *plural* over the presumably unified modern psyche, and the radical *otherness* of the collective unconscious rather than the hegemonic ego. We will show that each of these positions was subversive vis-à-vis modern, secular psychology.[21]

The Religious Psyche

Over the past five centuries, the religious language used to describe the self has shifted from the medieval psyche to the modern psyche, which is explained without use of religious discourse.[22] The ancient psyche was contained within a sacral order, but the modern self is not.[23] Pathology in modern terms is then a consequence of early trauma, faulty conditioning, or biological abnormalities — natural forces, not spiritual. The secular psyche is defined in terms of genetics, social conditioning, introjection of others, and so forth. The assumption guiding these notions is that the mind is best understood in terms of naturalism and positivism. When religion is referenced in psychology, it tends to be viewed as useful, as an

21. However, we are quick to admit that in certain respects, Jung did not transcend the modern ethos. His view of the collective conscious as possessing universal symbols and images and his preoccupation with the individual psyche reflect a modernist foundationalism. In modernist mode, ethics and morality remain innate for Jung. See Jung, *Civilization in Transition,* vol. 10 of *The Collected Works of C. G. Jung,* trans. R. F. C. Hull (New York: Pantheon, 1958), paras. 825-57.

22. Alvin Dueck, "Integration and Christian Scholarship," in *Integrating Psychology and Theology,* ed. Dueck, pp. ix-xxviii; and *The Secular Revolution,* ed. Christian Smith.

23. Philip Rieff, *My Life among the Deathworks: Illustrations of the Aesthetics of Authority* (Charlottesville: University of Virginia Press, 2006).

adaptive coping mechanism.[24] Religious symbols in human experience are viewed more as curios than as possibly numinous. Knowledge of the human self is generated not from sacred texts but from carefully controlled research with generalizable findings.

Modern psychology denuded the religious psyche, but Jung did not. For him, spirituality was integral to personhood, but few took notice of his insistence on this. While Freud construed *libido* as sexual energy, Jung viewed libido as *pneuma,* spirit. He investigated the psychological meaning of the Lord's Supper, the Trinity, and theodicy. He pointed to the psychological effects of the numinous and the spiritual power of the symbolic, of images and of ritual.[25]

Jung was concerned that the repository of psychologically significant religious images and symbols in the collective human reservoir had reached a low ebb in the twentieth century. His reaction was to develop a psychology that would help to "re-establish connection to the truths of religious symbols by finding their equivalents in our own psychic experience."[26] With the virtual disappearance of institutions as the containers of religious sensibilities, the only hope was the spiritually alive individual. However, Jung argued, spirituality within the individual was in need of a new interpretative framework. God could come to us in symbols, dreams, and fantasy, a kind of natural revelation that the Reformed tradition refers to as "common grace."[27]

Neurosis for Jung included not taking seriously the religious instinct of the psyche, resulting in a loss of meaning. It was Jung who, in a conversation with the founders of Alcoholics Anonymous, suggested that alco-

---

24. Joel James Shuman and Keith G. Meador, *Heal Thyself: Spirituality, Medicine, and the Distortion of Christianity* (Oxford: Oxford University Press, 2003); and Alvin Dueck, "Thick Patients, Thin Therapy, and a Prozac God," *Theology, News, and Notes* 53 (2005): 4-6.

25. See Jung, *Psychology and Religion: West and East,* vol. 11 of *The Collected Works of C. G. Jung,* trans. R. F. C. Hull (New York: Pantheon, 1958).

26. Ulanov, "Jung and Religion: The Opposing Self," in *The Cambridge Companion to Jung,* ed. Polly Young-Eisendrath and Terence Dawson (Cambridge: Cambridge University Press, 1997), p. 297.

27. Richard J. Mouw, *He Shines in All That's Fair: Culture and Common Grace* (Grand Rapids: William B. Eerdmans, 2001).

holism was a spiritual issue.[28] Jung warned therapists of the presence and power of evil in the context of culture and psychotherapy. Jung's fundamental openness to spirituality and to religious traditions encourages therapists to "mind spirituality."[29] He speaks our language: the cure of the soul *(cura animarum).*

Reviewing Jung's early life provides insight into the kind of spirituality that he eventually affirmed. A particularly significant influence on Jung was his religious upbringing, especially in the context of early experiences with his parents. Eight of Jung's paternal uncles were members of the clergy, and his earliest playgrounds were on church property. From his father's side of the family, Jung received the formal religious education of a Swiss Christian youth. However, Jung experienced his mother as emotionally unpredictable and, at times, frightening — in stark contrast to the religious stability of his father. His maternal grandfather was more at home with mystical and mysterious religious phenomena. These opposing influences resulted in irreconcilable beliefs and emotions within Jung, which would later be reflected in his theory of the psyche.[30]

Jung experienced a duality in his later academic education that paralleled his childhood religious experiences. His professors thoroughly believed in positivistic science. It was in this context that Jung came to appreciate the empirical sciences, which informed his early work with clinical case histories, diagnoses, and the formulation of projective tests. Contrasting with positivistic philosophy was Romanticism, the rise of which offered Jung a rich alternative that catered to the more spiritual elements of his personality. Alongside medical texts, he devoured the philosophical works of thinkers greatly influenced by the Romantic movement, including Immanuel Kant, Georg Wilhelm Hegel, Arthur

28. Jung, in a letter to Bill Wilson, January 30, 1961. See "Spiritus contra Spiritum: The Bill Wilson/C. G. Jung Letters: The Roots of the Society of Alcoholics Anonymous," *Parabola* 12 (1987): 68.

29. Randall Lehmann Sorenson, *Minding Spirituality* (Hillsdale, N.J.: Analytic Press, 2004).

30. For example, the *coniunctio oppositorum,* interpreted as the union of opposites, was a pivotal component for healthy psychological functioning in his model of the psyche.

Schopenhauer, and Friedrich Nietzsche.[31] These opposing influences, learned academically in both childhood and adulthood, help us to understand the persistent bifurcation that Jung felt at the core of his soul. He expressed this internal split by providing each half with a name.[32] "Number 1" reflected the rationalism of his Reformed upbringing, as well as the exacting positivism of his academic education. "Number 2," on the other hand, revealed the dark underbelly of his soul. It was this dimension of Jung's personality that was interested in Romantic thought, mysticism, and the darker aspects of human existence.

Despite the pervasive influence of Christian thought during Jung's youth, his views on religion departed some distance from those of his parents. His views also differed greatly from those held by the father of psychoanalysis, Sigmund Freud. Freud interpreted religion as fulfilling infantile wishes for the soothing presence of a parent, given the excessive demands of the cultural superego.[33] For Jung, however, religion held healing potential for the psyche. He saw religion as providing the myths and images necessary for the transformation of a fragmented psyche.

This is not to say that Jung thought of religion in utilitarian terms. Rather, fundamental to Jung's entire project was the assumption that the human person is essentially a religious being, a claim unprecedented among the dominant psychological theorists of the twentieth century. However, the view of the person as quintessentially spiritual has been asserted repeatedly in the history of Christian thought, notably by theological figures such as Paul, Augustine, and John Calvin.[34]

---

31. Such influences include Kant's *a priori* categories of thought on Jung's concept of archetypes, Hegel's dialectical method on Jung's concept of reconciling intrapsychic opposites, and Nietzsche's understanding of tragedy on Jung's concern with the darker elements of human psychology.

32. Jung, *Memories, Dreams, Reflections,* trans. Richard and Clara Winston (New York: Vintage Books, 1961), pp. 45-46.

33. Freud, *The Future of an Illusion* (New York: Norton, 1928/1989).

34. See Paul, Romans 1:18-31; Augustine, *Confessions* (Oxford: Oxford University Press, 1991); and Calvin, *Institutes of the Christian Religion,* trans. Henry Beveridge (Grand Rapids: William B. Eerdmans, 1953), 1.1.1-3.

The Plural Psyche

Is the human soul an indivisible unity or a conflicted plurality? From Aristotle onward, the soul has been assumed to be indivisible:

> Some say that the soul is divisible and that one part of it thinks, another desires. What is it then which holds the soul together, if naturally divisible? Assuredly, it is not the body: on the contrary, the soul seems rather to hold the body together; at any rate when the soul is gone, the body dissolves into air and decays. If, then, the unity of the soul were due to some other thing, that other thing would be, properly speaking, soul. Why not attribute unity to the soul?[35]

Many centuries later, one of the architects of modern psychology, John Locke, averred that identity meant the sameness of the self over time.[36] The autonomous Enlightenment soul is singular and unitary. Since the power of the soul is thought which is immaterial, it follows that the soul is a unity. French existentialist Jean-Paul Sartre denied the idea of division within the person, believing that such a concept would lay the groundwork for excuses to deny the individual's absolute freedom and responsibility.[37] The unity of the soul is an idea clearly found in some parts of the Christian tradition. After all, did not God provide each body with an individual, immaterial substance called the soul? For mainstream positivist psychologists and religionists, a divided consciousness in the form of pathological dissociation or demonic possession is anathema. The unconscious, which presumably influences human behavior, is then for the empirical psychologist a myth. While there are negative and positive forces that shape us, they do not constitute sub-personalities within us.

What then is this plurality? Of what does it consist? Jung describes as separate psychological realities the ego and the unconscious, the shadow and archetypal experiences, the masculine and the feminine

---

35. Aristotle, *De Anima* (Oxford: Clarendon Press, 1961), vol. 1, 411b.

36. Locke, *An Essay Concerning Human Understanding* (New York: Dover Publications, 1959).

37. Sartre, *Of Human Freedom* (New York: Philosophical Library, 1967).

within one individual. Like Freud before him, Jung viewed the psyche as struggling with contending forces, incompatible parts, opposing personalities. Jung's plural psyche is composed of the complexes, which are "feeling-toned groups of representations"[38] that emerge from an interaction between the unconscious and conscious experience. The complex is the basis of Jung's speaking of the "little people," complexes that have a certain amount of coherence and autonomy. Complexes are "splinter psyches."[39] Rilke once observed that "shattered beings are best represented by bits and pieces."[40] Jung believed that the diversity within was not necessarily pathological but a potential gift. This understanding of the psyche as plural is one more way in which Jung responded pastorally and prophetically to the presumption of modernity.

We begin our analysis of the cast of characters with the ego, which, for Jung, "constitutes the centre of my field of consciousness and appears to possess a high degree of continuity and identity."[41] Although the ego generally emerges in the third or fourth year of life, one spends the first half of life developing the "heroic" ego, which through persistent acts of striving seeks to "make it" in the world. "The ego is the subject of all successful attempts at adaptation so far as these are achieved by the will."[42] Further, the ego is typically identified with certain dominant personality traits that emerge out of this relationship with external reality, such as introversion and extroversion, thinking and feeling, sensation and intuition. In all of this we have an excellent description of the modern ego, autonomous and unencumbered.

Jung proceeded a step further with another psychological reality. Despite being the center of consciousness, the ego discovers its own limita-

38. Jung, *Experimental Researches*, vol. 2 of *The Collected Works of C. G. Jung*, trans. R. F. C. Hull (Princeton: Princeton University Press, 1973), paras. 329, 352.

39. Jung, *The Structure and Dynamics of the Psyche*, vol. 8 of *The Collected Works of C. G. Jung*, trans. R. F. C. Hull (Princeton: Princeton University Press, 1970), para. 253.

40. Rilke, quoted in Zygmunt Bauman, *Postmodern Ethics* (Oxford: Blackwell, 1993), p. 1.

41. Jung, *Psychological Types*, vol. 6 of *The Collected Works of C. G. Jung*, trans. R. F. C. Hull (Princeton: Princeton University Press, 1974), para. 706.

42. Jung, *The Archetypes and the Collective Unconscious*, vol. 9a of *The Collected Works of C. G. Jung*, trans. R. F. C. Hull (Princeton: Princeton University Press, 1969), para. 11.

tions when confronted with the unknown, the unconscious. It experiences itself as being "moved" by a potent internal force. Two levels are involved in this internal subversion of ego control. One is the personal unconscious, which contains those inferior or undeveloped elements of the personality that have failed to be fully integrated into conscious awareness. The second level involves a transpersonal or collective unconscious that houses an inner experience of the transcendent, a call to more integrated ways of being. This confrontation with the transcendent imposes upon the ego a demand to submit to something higher than itself. Healthy psychological development, according to Jung, requires an increased capacity for conscious awareness of those inferior and transcendent powers that appear within the psyche. In Hegelian fashion, the ego contains the opposites and engenders a new creative alternative. The reason for midlife crises, according to Jung, is that people spend so much time in the first half of their lives with an external orientation to the world, seeking success, that they fail to acknowledge the call from their non-ego parts to greater wholeness.

Those inferior personality traits submerged in unconsciousness Jung called the shadow, "the thing a person has no wish to be,"[43] "the sum of all those unpleasant qualities"[44] from which one attempts to hide. The shadow, that which we reject in ourselves, may contain elements of evil and also highly positive elements. However, when the negative is not acknowledged, the shadow can develop a life of its own as a subpersonality and be unconsciously projected onto an object or person in the external world. The failure to own one's shadow is demonstrated in a case where, for example, a pastor outwardly shows vehement disdain for pornography, fighting to rid the world of such "filth"; yet this same individual may simultaneously be fantasizing about pornography or having a secret affair. While certainly not denying the reality of evil or the right of individuals to protest against it, Jung was concerned when someone obsessed about what he or she saw as particularly "wrong" behavior. The

43. Jung, *The Practice of Psychotherapy*, vol. 16 of *The Collected Works of C. G. Jung*, trans. R. F. C. Hull (Princeton: Princeton University Press, 1966), para. 470.

44. Jung, *Two Essays on Analytical Psychology*, vol. 7 of *The Collected Works of C. G. Jung*, trans. R. F. C. Hull (Princeton: Princeton University Press, 1966), p. 66n.

question arises: What evil do we deny in ourselves as we come to see it with such clarity in another? According to Jung, "everyone carries a shadow, and the less it is embodied in the individual's conscious life, the blacker and denser it is."[45] This psychological phenomenon highlights the importance of considering the "beam" in one's eye before addressing the "speck" in another's (Matt. 7:3).

We move now to an example of even greater plurality in the psyche as Jung saw it, the archetypal images. The archetypes constitute the collective unconscious, an inherited reservoir of images, wisdom, and surprises. In studying the diverse cultures of the world, Jung discovered common themes among varying myths and religious narratives. He argued, based upon Darwin's theory of evolution, that these reoccurring themes represented a psychological inheritance analogous to biologically based instincts. Jung used the term "archetype" to describe these emotion-laden images, which could constellate in complexes or sub-personalities.

In themselves, archetypes are devoid of any specific content, and require some symbol or image through which they can find concrete expression. An archetypal image is the means by which the unconscious finds cultural expression in the concrete experiences of conscious living. "The image is a condensed expression of the psychic situation as a whole."[46] Jung noted the various ways in which archetypal images can be expressed. For example, the circle, an image of completeness and infinity, has been used as a symbol depicting divinity and is reflective of the Self archetype. This image was used by Gustav Doré to depict Dante's encounter with God in *The Divine Comedy;* it is also used in Buddhism, in a complex circular pattern called a mandala. Sometimes archetypal images are expressed in religious narratives, such as the "death-rebirth" story. The process whereby one dies to an old identity only to be reborn into a new one is found in Christianity in the experience of baptism and resurrection. This religious enactment is correlated with psychological experience when the ego learns to forgo its assumed control of the world and surrender to the call of the Self.

45. Jung, *Psychology and Religion: West and East,* para. 131.
46. Jung, *Psychological Types,* para. 745.

Another plurality is that of the masculine and the feminine as psychological realities. This is a particularly potent archetype that individuals often fail to own. Jung calls this the soul-image. One's soul-image represents the dominant masculine or feminine orientation of the unconscious, and is portrayed as the mirror opposite of one's personality. Thus, for males, the soul-image is often personified as a woman, and for females, as a man. Soul-images are represented in mythology through certain "masculine" and "feminine" figures such as Hercules and Helen of Troy or, for more modern Hollywood examples, Brad Pitt and Meg Ryan. The plurality in the psyche involves play between masculine and feminine. Since the soul-image is experienced as a foreign and opposing entity to the ego, it lends itself to being frequently displaced unconsciously onto external reality, most often onto a person of the opposite sex. In such situations, erotic attractions often result in which the other is perceived as numinous, embodying all the features of one's soul-image. The psyche contains an internal drive toward wholeness that evokes this longing to be united with the opposite within itself. However, when the ego fails to recognize this internal calling, psychic energy is displaced onto a real other, male or female. The failure to recognize and identify our soul-image as emanating from the unconscious can result in utter disillusionment when we discover that the other does not match our archetypal fantasies. However, such crises present an opportunity to learn what qualities we lack in ourselves and are projecting outward. Hence, a man can come to know his more "feminine" qualities, while a woman can begin to integrate her unacknowledged "masculine" traits.

Other prominent personified images may shape our inner plurality. They approach us in the realms of mythology, dreams, and external day-to-day experiences in images that include the Wise Old Man/Woman, the Hero, and the Clown. To consider a popular example, the *Star Wars* movie series intentionally re-enacted a story based upon Jungian archetypes.[47]

47. George Lucas, the producer and director of *Star Wars,* was very much influenced by the ideas of cultural anthropologist Joseph Campbell, whose work was directly influenced by Jung's theory.

In the films, Luke Skywalker represents the personification of the Hero, Obi-Wan Kenobi embodies the Wise Old Man, and C-3PO and R2-D2 reflect the Clown archetype. The ominous figure of Darth Vader is the prototypical image of the Shadow, while the mystical notion of the Force, the ubiquitous creative energy of the universe, is an image of the god-archetype of the Self. Characters such as those found in *Star Wars* touch on reservoirs of energy deeper than the particular stories themselves. In other words, what elicits such affective engagement in these movies is the potent resonance the stories have with the collective psyche of a particular culture. They allow us to identify with the hero, the villain, or the source of wisdom found within our psyches. This also explains the fascination with mythic stories in films such as *Harry Potter, The Lord of the Rings, The Chronicles of Narnia,* and *The Da Vinci Code.* Each provides characters and scenarios that allow us to access parts of ourselves in our plural psyches.

Given this plethora of identities, the question naturally arises: What holds the psyche together? Jung called the lifelong struggle by the Self to integrate these various archetypal images and parts of the unconscious with the psyche "individuation." This is the process by which one seeks one's fullest actualization through the differentiation and integration of all parts of the psyche. Thus, the ego is divested of identification with any one particular element of the collective unconscious, while simultaneously accepting the presence of all the elements as part of the total psyche. Although individuation, with its emphasis on differentiation, is similar to the concept of individualism, the two are, in fact, very different for Jung: "Individualism means deliberately stressing and giving prominence to some supposed peculiarity, rather than to collective considerations and obligations. But individuation means precisely the better and more complete fulfillment of collective qualities."[48]

In this type of development, one is more fully actualized through a lifelong process of integrating a fragmented psyche. This healing of fragmented parts involves the reconciling of opposites. The psyche is always

48. Jung, *Two Essays on Analytical Psychology,* para. 267.

in a process of seeking reparation among these opposites, a union of unlike psychological qualities, sometimes symbolized in dreams by a mandala or in mythology as an androgynous figure.

For Jung, then, the psyche is plural — composed of many parts, each jostling the others for control. To acknowledge the plurality of identity is to recognize both one's brokenness and the possibility of growth. To accept this plurality is to realize that one does well to pastor this inner congregation of selves.[49] Christians should read Jung because he is a reminder of the structure of the sacralized soul.[50] The ancient Near Eastern psyche bears certain — though not complete — resemblances to the psyche described in Jung's work. Berger, citing Paul in the New Testament, states that "the 'inner person' is not some stable and durable interiority but rather an invisible eschatological identity (2 Cor. 4:16)."[51] Thus, Paul conceives of the unified identity of the individual as a future hope to be *achieved* and not as a reality to be assumed. This is not to suggest that the particularities of what that unity consists of are also the same across millennia, but there is enough semantic and practical overlap to suggest that Jung's thought may indeed be more commensurate with views of the ancient soul than contemporary psychologists imagine.

Otherness in the Psyche

This internal plurality leads to another pressing pastoral issue that Jung raises: the place of otherness within the psyche. Otherness can simply be defined as those elements of experience that escape the grasp of the comprehending ego. Otherness eludes conceptualization, yet is fundamental to human experience.

The modern ego, however, has been "growing" these past centuries. Now unencumbered by tradition, it revels in its uniqueness, autonomy,

---

49. See Alvin Dueck, *Between Jerusalem and Athens: Ethical Perspectives on Culture, Religion, and Psychotherapy* (Grand Rapids: Baker, 1995), chap. 11.

50. Klaus Berger, *Identity and Experience in the New Testament*, trans. Charles Muenchow (Minneapolis: Fortress Press, 2003).

51. Berger, *Identity and Experience in the New Testament*, p. 8.

and self-sufficiency.[52] This is an ego in control. The other person is perceived as an extension of one's self, as the same.[53] For the other person to be truly different is a threat. The mystery of the *other* is domesticated.

If the ego opens up in passive receptivity to the Self, fulfillment is possible, but the notions of passivity and receptivity disrupt our modern sensibilities. The modern psyche is an active, pragmatic agent, assimilating the world and accommodating when necessary. Experiences of surrendering, submission, or being confronted conflict with the modern individual's proclivity for autonomy. Yet it is exactly this hubris and its encounter with otherness that Jung described in detail. The experience of otherness, which upsets the rational ego, is the source and summit of psychological wholeness. Just as Jesus warns that those who seek to save their own life will lose it (Matt. 16:25), so Jung offers this pastoral response.

Jung's approach brings back into discussion in the field of psychology that singular experience of otherness. There is that within the psychic economy, the unconscious, which the rational ego fails to comprehend. Jung refers to the interior, transcendent power of the psyche, this experience of the "Not-I," as the *Self*. The Self plays a pivotal role in organizing the totality of psychological functioning. In Jung's words, the Self is

> . . . a construct that serves to express an unknowable essence which we cannot grasp as such, since by definition it transcends our powers of comprehension. It might equally well be called the "God within us." The beginnings of our whole psychic life seem to be inextricably rooted in this point, and all our highest and ultimate purposes seem to be striving toward it.[54]

Through the Self emerge god-images that reflect the presence of the divine within the psyche. However, modern individuals easily dismiss such experiences because of their faith in epistemologically reductionistic forms of reason — scientific materialism, for example. This has made

---

52. Taylor, *Sources of the Self*.

53. Emmanuel Levinas, *Otherwise Than Being; or, Beyond Essence,* trans. Alphonso Lingis (Boston: M. Nijhoff, 1981).

54. Jung, *Two Essays on Analytical Psychology,* para. 399.

them tone-deaf to the call of the transcendent. Jung recognized this propensity in the modern and feared the consequences for civilization of suppressing the divine voice.

Critical to the emergence of the Self is the de-centering of one's ego, a process that occurs when one is forced to confront the unknown parts of one's psyche through dreams, fantasies, and symptoms. The Self demands conversation between the conscious and the unconscious. In working through contradictions and personal failures, psychological healing and transformation can occur. This activity of the Self is what Jung called its transcendent function. By acting as a bridge between the conscious and the unconscious, the Self allows the individual to move beyond the one-sidedness of the dominant character traits expressed by the ego. In the agony of living, in suffering the contradictions of life, in this de-centering of the ego, a new attitude, a novel way of being emerges, which has become more psychologically integrated. Jung stated, "I consider it my task and duty to educate my patients and pupils to the point where they can accept the direct demand that is made upon them from within."[55] Linking otherness with Jung's concept of the Self, Ulanov states,

> The self makes itself known as a presence or entity that is other than the ego but has direct far-reaching personal effects upon the ego. By *other* here, I mean that which is felt as sufficiently different from the ego to be experienced as an objective "person" that addresses its purposes, demands, or needs to the ego, and yet that is so similar to the ego and connected with it that the ego feels personally affected by its presence.[56]

This concept of Self and its activity as a functioning transcendent offered Jung a useful hermeneutic for interpreting the expression of psychological phenomena as an internal drive toward wholeness and trans-

55. Jung, *Letters,* 2 vols., ed. G. Adler and A. Jaffé, trans. R. F. C. Hull (Princeton, N.J.: Princeton University Press, 1973 and 1975), vol. 1, 26 May 1945, p. 41.

56. Ann Ulanov, "The Self as Other," in *Carl Jung and Christian Spirituality,* ed. Robert L. Moore (New York: Paulist Press, 1988), p. 46.

formation, rather than as emanating purely from pathology. Hence, anxiety or depression should be understood as the Self seeking liberation from a tyrannical ego whose dominance may be actively promoting disintegration. Symptoms, then, are potentially a gift from the Self in the service of promoting wholeness.

For Jung, numinosity is often associated with emergence of the Self. "It seizes and controls the human subject, who is always rather its victim than its creator. The *numinosum* . . . is an experience of the subject independent of his will."[57] The receptivity of the ego to the numinous Self parallels the spiritual journey toward God as described by great mystics such as St. John of the Cross. As a bearer of the God-image, the numinous Self also resembles the Christian theological concept of the *imago Dei*.[58] Jung's clear identification of the Self with Judeo-Christian monotheism is evident in the response of some post-Jungians such as James Hillman, who posited that Hellenistic polytheism rather than monotheism is the appropriate foundation of the Self.[59] For Hillman, monotheism too easily slips into totalitarianism and a constriction of imagination. Jung's Self leans toward the unity implicit in oneness, monotheism.

Another distinctive characteristic of the biblical mentality noted by Berger that resembles Jung's thought is "a pronounced openness toward the dimension of the Other."[60] That which was sacred, holy, and wholly other spoke to the ancients and informed their experiences and identity. One should be cautious not to overstate the similarity between this notion of otherness found in Scripture and Jung's concept of the Self. However, in paving the way for transcendence to speak in the therapeutic context, contemporary religious psychologists have not opened such a wide path for a sacred order to speak to us as has Jung in his articulation of numinous experiences within psychic life. What Berger elucidates in the psychology of the New Testament, Jung intuited — but found absent in modernity. Jung can help us to recover a sacral psychology and draw out more clearly the call of God in Christ on the psyche.

57. Jung, *Psychology and Religion: West and East,* para. 6.
58. Jung, *Memories, Dreams, Reflections,* p. 382.
59. Hillman, *Archetypal Psychology* (Putnam, Conn.: Spring Publications, 2004).
60. Berger, *Identity and Experience in the New Testament,* p. 12.

So then, why should evangelicals read Jung? To summarize, we have suggested that Jung's critique of the effects of modernity is both prophetic and pastoral. Rather than simply accepting the secular self as a given, Jung created room for spirituality. Jung placed the complex plurality of the psyche in contrast to the monolithic ego that is still predominant in various contemporary psychological theories. He relativized the autonomous ego by suggesting that we are more fragmented than we realize and by pointing to the other in the psyche that is not reducible to what is familiar.

For religious psychologists enamored with modernity, Jung's approach should be experienced as offensive. Lecturing at Heidelberg in 1989, the Jewish philosopher Jacob Taubes commented, "I don't know anyone who is a Protestant who doesn't want to be modern."[61] In spite of its suspicion of modernity, conservative Christianity has imbibed more of modernity's ethos than it is aware — or willing to admit. In the early 1900s, conservative American Christianity reacted negatively to the rise of modernist thought. Today the adaptation to modernity is evident in conservative Christianity's openness to modernist methods in biblical studies and the creation of universal propositional theologies that are ahistorical and acultural.[62] Even the epistemology, Nancey Murphy has argued, is modernist, with its emphasis on representationalism and expressivism. The former is evident in the assumption that "Scripture provides precise and true accounts of supernatural realities."[63] While there are notable exceptions to this critique of conservative theologies, we would maintain that a careful reading of Jung's assessment of the modern psyche remains helpful.

61. Taubes, *The Political Theology of Paul,* ed. Aleida Assmann and Jan Assmann, trans. Dana Hollander (Stanford, Calif.: Stanford University Press, 2004), p. 84.

62. George Marsden, *Fundamentalism and American Culture: The Shaping of Twentieth-Century Evangelicalism, 1870-1925* (New York: Oxford University Press, 1980); Mark Noll, "Common-Sense Traditions and American Evangelical Thought," *American Quarterly* 37 (1985): 216-38; and R. Greer, *Mapping Postmodernism: A Survey of Christian Options* (Downers Grove, Ill.: InterVarsity Press, 2003).

63. Murphy, *Beyond Liberalism and Fundamentalism: How Modern and Postmodern Philosophy Set the Theological Agenda* (Valley Forge, Pa.: Trinity Press International, 1996), p. 97.

The Ulanov Essays

Ann Belford Ulanov is the Christiane Brooks Johnson Professor of Psychiatry and Religion at Union Theological Seminary, a psychoanalyst in private practice, and a member of the Jungian Psychoanalytic Association and of the International Association of Anayltical Psychology. She is the recipient of an honorary doctorate from Virginia Theological School and from the Loyola Graduate Department in Pastoral Counseling and from Christian Theological Seminary. She has also received the Distinguished Alumna Award from the Blanton/Peale Institute, the Vision Award from the National Association for the Advancement of Psychoanalysis, the Oskar Pfister Award from the American Psychiatric Association for Distinguished Work in Depth Psychology and Religion, and the Distinguished Contribution Award from the American Association of Pastoral Counselors for Distinguished Work in Depth Psychology and Religion.

From the very beginning of her professional career, Ulanov has engaged in issues of integrating Christian faith and theology with depth psychology.[64] In her essays here, she invites the reader to participate in the healing transformation of psyche and soul that can occur in the space between psychology and theology. However, as Ulanov argues, there is a Christian fear of the psyche that impedes conversation between these two fields.

Ulanov offers us a bridge to traverse between Jung's thought and Christian faith. In building this bridge, Ulanov resists the temptation to collapse one mode of discourse into another. Rather, she allows a legitimate space in which honest, authentic conversation can occur. In another work, Ulanov reminded her readers that each dialogue partner must maintain a separate identity, while simultaneously being changed by the interaction. She characterizes herself as standing in a parallel manner between psychology and theology and between the ego and the Self, encouraging conversation.[65] Her objective is not to make Christian-

64. Ulanov, *The Feminine in Jungian Psychology and in Christian Theology* (Evanston, Ill.: Northwestern University Press, 1971).

65. Ulanov, *Spiritual Aspects of Clinical Work* (Einsiedeln, Switzerland: Daimon, 2004), pp. 40-41.

ity acceptable to Jungian perspectives, and she does not simply baptize Jung so that he will be acceptable to evangelicals. Each has a contribution to make.

Depth psychology is a corrective to an overly spiritualized faith, pointing to the everydayness, the messiness, of experience and incarnation. But the Christian faith is our mother tongue, and it determines our identity. Ulanov does not hesitate to suggest where Jung overstepped his self-proclaimed boundaries for sticking strictly with the psychological. At the same time, she shows that Christians can benefit from this conversation with Jung as well, helping us to acknowledge some of the blind spots that often keep us from living out more fully our core convictions. In the following essays, Ulanov addresses three major issues: reductionism, femininity and the shadow, and God-images. We will briefly review these central concerns to help to provide some context for her discussion.

Reductionism

Christian faith contains a surfeit of meaning and mystery that no single theory can capture. In her first essay, Ulanov addresses reasons for the fear of the psyche — psychological reductionism among Christians in general, and evangelicals in particular. Ulanov suggests that this fear partly concerns a perceived translation of Christianity into psychological terms. When one speaks about the rich biblical narrative in terms of a simpler and supposedly more acceptable schema, the fear naturally arises that Christianity will not fit on the Procrustean bed without some mutilation. Some have been concerned that Jungian notions of universal archetypes and individuation have been used to reinterpret faith.

What is overlooked, Ulanov suggests, is that Jung was on an intense spiritual journey, as all of us are, to find an authentic way to respond to the real God. In this analysis we find that Jung provides a way to think about Christianity as embodied in human experience. The psyche becomes a medium through which God speaks to us within the concrete, tangible realities of our day-to-day existence. Recognizing the inextricable psychological element in our spiritual journey does not negate or subvert the interpretative role of dogma and history, but adds to it another dimension.

If this is so, we are implored to concern ourselves with the medium through which God's voice is heard. That medium, our psyche, is conditioned by personal and collective histories. In discerning the voice of God, we inevitably must ask ourselves what extraneous elements attach to our faith that detract from an encounter with the Transcendent. God is one who speaks through the psyche as well as through revelation, and here in human experience is where we meet, or refuse to meet, the living God.

The Shadow and the Feminine

In her second essay, Ulanov addresses those parts of the psyche and of our faith that are often left undeveloped — namely, the shadow and the feminine. These are themes she has addressed in several previous works.[66] Jung pointed to what appeared to be the dark element of the divine. What does one do with those darker images of God? Since we come to know God through our psyche, we must, Ulanov suggests, be prepared for the muck of our own inner stable in which the divine is born. Inherited with the pure gracious gift of God's self are the unacceptable parts of our lives that get attached to our views of God.

Another focus of this essay concerns feminine aspects of our faith. Ulanov suggests that we think of ourselves in more feminine terms as modeled by Mary, and as suggested by Scripture texts that link the believer to Christ as his bride.[67] This metaphor has also been used to express Yahweh's relationship with Israel (Isaiah 62:5). As the church, we house God as Mary carried Jesus in her womb. This maternal language,

66. See Ulanov, *The Feminine in Jungian Psychology and in Christian Theology*; Ulanov, *Receiving Woman: Studies in the Psychology and Theology of the Feminine* (Philadelphia: Westminster Press, 1981); Ann Belford Ulanov and Barry Ulanov, *The Witch and the Clown: Two Archetypes of Human Sexuality* (Wilmette, Ill.: Chiron Publications, 1987); and Ann Belford Ulanov and Barry Ulanov, *Transforming Sexuality: The Archetypal World of Anima and Animus* (Boston: Shambhala, 1994).

67. Revelation 19:7-10; Matthew 9:15; and John 3:29.

used since the early church, provides a helpful corrective to more paternal approaches, which have tended toward theological intellectualization and propositional truths. The feminine mode of being, conversely, invites us into more embodied and communal elements of our faith, to become receptive vessels for the Holy Other, who fills us individually and communally.

God-Images

In her third essay, Ulanov details the role of God-images and their relationship to a living faith. The topic of God's image in the human soul emerges repeatedly in Ulanov's writing, both in her individual works and in works that she wrote with her late husband, Barry Ulanov. In a work dedicated to the Jungian concept of the transcendent function, Ulanov shows how the transcendent appears in clinical work, how to be sensitive to this presence in dreams and symptoms, and how the presence of the transcendent informs the encounter between therapist and client.[68] She has also examined the nature of God-images that surface in prayers, dreams, and experiences of the holy.[69] The Ulanovs coauthored a work dealing with the centrality of imagination in the spiritual life, particularly with regard to preaching, prayer, teaching, counseling, and politics.[70]

According to Ulanov, there exists a space between subjective and objective God-images. Our personal God-image may even deviate greatly from those received by tradition. However, what lies within this space is a living God whose presence is mediated through a dynamic, dialectic interplay between our schemas and a simultaneous separation from them. Jung's theory of opposites and the psyche's transcendent function help us to think psychologically about the activity occurring within this space and to pay special attention to its healing properties. If we struggle

68. Ulanov, *The Functioning Transcendent: A Study in Analytical Psychology* (Wilmette, Ill.: Chiron Publications, 1996).

69. Ulanov, *Picturing God* (Einsiedeln, Switzerland: Daimon Verlag, 2002).

70. Ann Belford Ulanov and Barry Ulanov, *The Healing Imagination* (Einsiedeln, Switzerland: Daimon Verlag, 1999).

to go on praying and being faithful, Ulanov says, we navigate the inevitable breakdown and reconstruction of all of our images, because nothing finite can encompass the infinite, unoriginated God.

ALVIN DUECK *and*
BRIAN W. BECKER

Essays by Ann Belford Ulanov

The Christian Fear of the Psyche

Fear of Jung

Carl Jung thought of himself as an empiricist, studying facts. If he had a next life on earth, he said he wanted to be a natural scientist: "Research in the natural sciences, yes, that I could imagine as the content of a new life."[1] Yet Jung is noted as the depth psychologist who was involved his whole life long with religion, and particularly the Christian faith in which he found himself embedded. By the end of his life, Jung worked out his own revisioning of the spiritual journey and how we are to be serving God. He reached his solution, one that commands our respect even if or when we disagree with his conclusions; for these are not intellectual summations but his response to the call, the *vocatio* that summons the whole person.

People of faith often fear Jung's work. We must ask why and try to answer the dread his approach inspires. Chief among objections to his work is the fear that he translates Christian faith into psychological terms, that he is guilty of reductionism. In place of God, we find his notion of the Self archetype; in place of responding to the promptings of the Holy Spirit, we seek the promptings of the unconscious; in place of the guidance of defined dogma, we find symbols opening to the undefined All of the transcendent that cannot be captured in finite terms.

1. Aniela Jaffé, *Was C. G. Jung a Mystic?* (Einsiedeln, Switzerland: Daimon, 1989), p. 112.

31

In responding to those objections, I am not defending Jung. He needs no defense; his work stands on its own feet and displays its own merit. Instead, I am standing in between his work and the Christian faith tradition, looking in both directions, speaking now about the psyche as I have come to perceive and understand it, and now in the same way about our shared faith. I see Jung as a man and a clinician dealing in all his work with the numinous God. He struggled mightily to reach his own interpretation of the Christian myth, to create a response that made sense to him and commanded his devotion. His was an intense spiritual journey to make God real and to survive the reality of God.

Each of us, too, seeks to find our way individually and together in community to a real path to the real God. We cannot piggyback on Jung's solution but must reach our own. Where we differ from the tradition and try to go back to it and conform, or try to split away from it and forget a spiritual path — this will not do. We want to stay faithful to the way shown to us that we both receive and create. I believe there is no future for the church without including the psyche, especially the unconscious. I would add the arts as well. Both of these help us with the necessary conversation with the depths, and in our own spiritual formation.

The Self as God?

Let us take up the objection of reductionism. I like best this reply from Jung: "I cannot even replace a button with my imagination, so how could I possibly replace God?!" The Self archetype cannot replace God. The Self is that second center deep in the whole psyche, collecting into one potential unity the ordinary complexes of the psyche (ego, shadow, anima/us, persona). The Self also includes the complexes that disorder us (for example, inferiority, or father-boundness), as well as the perverse pull of addictions, suicidal urges, and homicidal eruptions of rage. Jung says the Self can never take the place of God.[2] However, he also says that Self-

---

2. Jung, *Good and Evil in Analytical Psychology,* vol. 10 of *The Collected Works of C. G. Jung,* trans. R. F. C. Hull (New York: Pantheon, 1959/1964), para. 874.

images and God-images are often indistinguishable. He is looking from the inside, from within the numinous experience where we know, are convinced, that a transcendent presence addresses us. From that perspective, it is hard to tell if God is outside us or inside us or both, but that is not the first question on our minds. The first questions usually are these: Can I survive this? Will it kill me? Am I crazy? Who is this! What does it ask of me? How am I to live with thee? Along with these come a cascading of affect, imagery, and body pulsing that tumbles together in a profound pouring out of devotion.

How we respond to such experiences of the transcendent shapes how we do our clinical work. Jung dwelt in the experience, not abstracted from it, and, to find his way spiritually, he needed to relate to God right there in the rough-and-tumble of human life. He said the abstract God "beyond all human experience leaves me cold. We do not affect each other. But if I know that he is a powerful impulse of my soul, at once I must concern myself with him. . . ."[3] Does this mean God is only an impulse of our soul? No; certainly not. But it does mean we must widen our perception of this presence in every person we counsel, every family we treat, and every group therapy we lead, as well as every night in our own prayers.

Jung responded to such experiences that befell him with fear as well as attraction. He sensed they laid upon him a duty in his work. He said that despite our "fear of primordial experience, I consider it my task and duty to educate my patients and pupils to the point where they can accept the direct demand made upon them from within."[4] From his study of early Christian writings, he said, "I have gained a deep and indelible impression of how dreadfully serious an experience of God is. It will be no different today."[5]

More than three decades of clinical work have brought me to the

3. Jung, "Commentary on the Secret of the Golden Flower," in *Alchemical Studies,* vol. 13 of *The Collected Works of C. G. Jung,* trans. R. F. C. Hull (Princeton: Princeton University Press, 1929/1967), paras. 412-413.

4. Jung, *Letters,* 2 vols., ed. G. Adler and A. Jaffé (Princeton: Princeton University Press, 1973 and 1975), vol. 1, letter of May 26, 1945, p. 41.

5. Jung, *Letters,* vol. 1 (1973), p. 41.

clarity that the Self, in Jung's jargon, is not God, but is that within us that knows about God. Another way to put it is to say that the Self in us is one of the complexes that make up the psyche, and it functions as a bridge to reality that transcends the whole psyche.[6] Thus, in actual clinical work I find myself in a stance similar to the one I take here, between Jung on the one hand and the faith tradition on the other, looking in both directions, and enunciating a position discovered and crafted, indeed growing from psychological as well as theological roots. In the clinical session, I am occupied in the space between ego and Self, the ego for Jung being the center of consciousness, and the Self that second center of the whole psyche, including ego, including conscious and unconscious. The ego has to do with functioning in the here and now and with the recovery of lost functions; the Self has to do with the whole of reality, both within and without, and with the ages, the human story under the light of eternity.

Listening to a person speaking in distress, I am hearing both what the ego needs, wants, and despairs of recovering; and what the Self may be engineering. The two things are not always the same, as is best illustrated in my book *The Wizards' Gate: Picturing Consciousness,* which tells the story of a woman finishing her analysis who, with her whole life opening before her, was struck down by a malignant brain tumor.[7] The book is about the last year and a half of her life, and how we worked to face into her death. Her ego, her conscious self, opposed death and felt outrage and grief for a life lost. Her unconscious in dramatic terms went on working to build up and support her becoming whole, with all the parts of herself brought into her experience of dying. I was stunned by one of the last things she said, not long before she died: "It was all worth it."

On a less dramatic note (but no less important for another woman's living, in contrast here to the former woman's dying), this double perspective occasioned a shift from what another patient called "deadness," which she experienced as a blank space where she dropped out and dis-

6. Ulanov, *Spiritual Aspects of Clinical Work* (Einsiedeln, Switzerland: Daimon, 2004), chaps. 12-13.

7. Ulanov, *The Wizards' Gate: Picturing Consciousness* (Einsiedeln, Switzerland: Daimon, 1994).

appeared from contact with herself and others, to what she called "aliveness." This shift was a long time in coming and took a lot of work. She functioned very successfully in her job as a religious professional, had achieved a happy marriage, and had good relations with her own children and her stepchildren. An outward observer would wonder why she persisted in therapy, but inwardly she was filled with paralyzing dread in the face of this blank space that always hovered near. Looking from the ego perspective, I would attend to the paralysis and how to deal with it and not succumb. Looking from the Self perspective, I would be asking: What is being engineered here? What does the blank space want? It required all her courage to face and enter into the unknown that she experienced as deeply threatening, and all her courage to depend on our analytical relationship to steady and support her, a dependence she needed to recognize and accept.

From the Self perspective, the symptom is a messenger, heralding a bigger way to live, even though we experience that symptom as threatening ego breakdown. In this example, the "blank space" symptom was hard to talk about because there was nothing there, hardly even words. This woman and I were forced to abandon customary modes of communication and seek new ones. The timing was slower, the information given in nudges, body gestures, hints, intuitions, and odd imagery. The clinical question shifted from how to survive deadness to how to overcome it, fix it, mend it, understand it, trace its origins. Then we moved to new questions: how to enter it, meet it, engage it, listen to it. The clinical question shifted from understanding and recovery to following the unknown to a new place. The new clinical question became how to house aliveness, to attend to how it manifests every day. As this woman put it, "I want to let myself live into that aliveness."

From this new perspective, we see deadness as a defense — not a symptom, not the problem. I have even seen lifelong depression, with still another patient, reveal itself finally as a defense, a protection against unbearable vulnerability, rather than an intractable condition. This perspective gives the clinician a crowbar to leverage the dead depression away from the vulnerability it is shielding, to give breathing room to the vulnerability — and then the person can grow.

The Unconscious as Holy Spirit?

My response to the second objection leveled at Jung — that we pay attention to the promptings of the unconscious instead of those of the Spirit — is to remind us of something we already know. God can speak through the psyche just as much as through Scripture, historical events, the worshipping community, love relationships, poetry, political movements, and whatever else. God can reach us through anything at any time. Nothing is too low to be a vehicle for God's mercy, as the muck of the stable in which Christ is born declares. What we repeatedly find hard to digest is that God is transcendent, infinite, unoriginated, and untamable. We want to corral the overwhelming numinosity of the Holy in grand but domesticated containers, even rules, ethical maxims, like Job receiving wholeheartedly the law given by Yahweh. We dread being put in Job's position of asking, But you gave the law, so why are you not abiding by it? Job is the best of us, asking his heartfelt question out of his suffering; and he is able to bear the answer of a new vision of God, bigger than the law, seeing that the transcendent God really is transcendent and is the author of the law.

The hermeneutic point here is that depth psychology adds another line of interpretation to the accustomed ones of historical, sociological, and literary methods of interpreting texts — namely, numinous moments. The new line of interpretation to be recognized is the fact of the psyche. In whatever ways we may interpret, we always do it in and through the human psyche. The new point is simply to recognize this and to cease to be afraid of it, which is what Jung means, I believe, when he says, "God has never spoken to [us] except in and through the psyche, and the psyche understands it. . . ."[8] The unconscious is another medium through which God reaches us.[9] Thus, just as we will ponder a passage in the Bible, we will also ponder a dream that strikes right to the heart. The Spirit that brings us the things of God blows freely where it will; it sur-

8. Jung, *Letters,* vol. 1 (1973), August 15, 1938, p. 98.
9. Jung, *Symbols of Transformation,* vol. 5 of *The Collected Works of C. G. Jung,* trans. R. F. C. Hull (Princeton: Princeton University Press, 1912/1967), para. 95.

rounds us and speaks from above and from below. The unconscious can be a medium of the Spirit reaching to us from the bottom up, so to speak, from down in the midst of the matter of things, as well as from the heights of inspired Scripture.

Symbols over Dogma?

In response to the criticism that Jung privileges symbols over dogma, we must remember his deep respect for dogma as the shared dream of humanity, crafted by countless minds over centuries. Jung counsels those of us to whom religious experience happens to remember that *religio,* that attitude of attentive consideration of transcendent factors, also binds us back, both personally and communally.[10] Such experience binds us personally back down to the primordial depths of our being, to being as it makes itself known to us. We may never understand such experiences; we may, like Mary, ponder them in our hearts for many years, but we dare not perjure such experiences, that is, pretend that they did not happen, or that they did not strike into us with ultimate significance. I like what Russian Orthodox Archbishop Anthony Bloom says about God: that God is prepared to be outside our life, and "prepared to take it up completely as a cross, but He is not prepared to be simply part of our life."[11]

We must also bind such experiences back into our community, for they loom out of us, and others will ask, "What has happened?" We dare not deny it, for such a secret isolates us and can even lead to madness. Such consultation with others, and the reading of the fathers and mothers of faith in history, help us in working over the meanings of the parable that gripped us, the numinous image that arrested us, the Eucharist that fed us. Dogma is made up of images spontaneously arriving, images like the Virgin Birth, the God-Man, the Trinity. The creed

10. Jung, *Psychology and Religion: West and East,* vol. 11 of *The Collected Works of C. G. Jung,* trans. R. F. C. Hull (New York: Pantheon, 1938/1958). See also Jung, *Letters,* vol. 1 (1973), January 13, 1948, p. 487.

11. Bloom, *Beginning to Pray* (New York: Paulist Press, 1970), p. 6.

and doctrines are chock full of such images. For Jung, image language is not opposed to faith, but is best suited to faith, better than theories we construct that come from our conscious efforts. Images come from the whole person, conscious and unconscious. Central to their power to move us is our recognition that we do not invent them; they address us and open us and bring with them a dimension of reality that transcends us.[12]

The image lies at the heart of the symbol, and symbol lies at the heart of faith, as we celebrate in every recitation of creed or ritual action. Image usually connotes the visual, but for some of us the other senses play the major role. A symbol may speak to hearing, as in the encounters of Yahweh with Moses — the voice coming from the bush, the words spoken in response to Moses' question, "Who should I say sent me?" It may be smell, as saints speak of the fragrance of Christ's nearness. It may be texture, as suggested by the enfolding well of darkness that is the apex of the spiritual journey for such greats as Gregory of Nyssa and St. Bernard of Clairvaux. It may even be taste, as is repeated in every Eucharist meal. A powerful symbol may include all the bodily senses that transform into what the mystics call the senses of the soul.

For Jung, the symbol is the best possible expression for something unknown or unknowable; it cannot be better expressed in any other way. A religious symbol is a living thing that brings us into the aliveness of that to which it points, opening us at the deepest levels of our being, as both the primitive common factor we share and the highest possible form of its expression.[13] The cross that stands for physical pain from which there is no rescue, for a humiliating death of ignominy, for abandonment by one's neighbors and one's God — it touches all of us at a deep level, whether or not we believe in it. Yet its spiritual significance reaches the highest order, expressing the cosmic interpenetration of

12. Jung, *Psychology and Religion,* paras. 81-82. See also Jung, *Memories, Dreams, Reflections,* ed. Aniela Jaffé, trans. Richard and Clara Winston (New York: Pantheon, 1963), pp. xff., 336.

13. Jung, *Psychological Types* (Princeton: Princeton University Press, 1971), para. 816; see also Ulanov, *The Feminine in Christian Theology and Jungian Philosophy* (Evanston, Ill.: Northwestern University Press, 1971), chap. 5.

heaven and earth, and representing the Tree of Life, from whose roots flow the four rivers of paradise and the four cardinal directions that are united at the fifth point of the cross's center. The cross's wood was thought in medieval times to be taken from the Tree of Knowledge, the cause of the Fall, which becomes in the crucifixion the instrument of redemption given in Christ's sacrifice that brings salvation.[14]

This understanding of symbol leads to the heart of what I have called the Christian fear of the psyche.[15] Jung emphasizes something that religious tradition has announced all along and that the mystics have explored in detail: that from the heart of reality, called Father, streams forth the nub of being, the very heart of the heart, called the Son. The two are the same substance; the one who streams forth is begotten, not made, and comes to us in history in the person of Jesus to lead us to discover that that which dwells at the heart of reality also dwells at the heart of each one of us and all of us together. The mystic Jan Van Ruysbroeck tells us that this sparkling stone of the Son standing forth from the Father comes to give us our very own name, known forever to the heart of reality.[16] Hadewijch of Brabant says the flame of God's love leaps up in us when the abyss of God meets the abyss of our soul.[17] St. Teresa of Ávila puts it more bluntly still: When we go into the interior castle of our self with its many mansions,[18] we find waiting for us at the center His Majesty, thus confirming Augustine's assertion *viderim me, viderim te,* "to know myself is to know you." This astounding proclamation is declared a scandal to the Jews and a stumbling block to the Greeks, and amounts to what I call the Christian fear of the psyche.

Experience of the theological fact of Jesus Christ comes to us

---

14. J. C. Cooper, *An Illustrated Encyclopedia of Traditional Symbols* (London: Thames & Hudson, 1978), p. 46.

15. Ulanov, *Picturing God* (Einsiedeln, Switzerland: Daimon, 1986/2002), pp. 5-23.

16. Van Ruysbroeck, "The Book of the Sparkling Stone," in *Medieval Netherlands Religious Literature,* trans. and ed. E. Colledge (New York: London House & Maxwell, 1965), p. 95.

17. Hadewijch of Brabant, *The Complete Works,* trans. Mother Columba Hart (Mahwah, N.J.: Paulist Press, 1980), pp. 60, 86.

18. St. Teresa of Ávila, *The Interior Castle,* in *The Complete Works of St. Teresa,* vol. 2, trans. and ed. E. Allison Peers (London: Sheed & Ward, 1957).

through the psyche, as does all experience. We have a better time accepting its coming through the body, though that can sometimes be so astounding that we can hardly believe it. Body means definite form, limited, finite, here in Pasadena, in New York City, in our particular lives with their set of chores, taxes, illnesses, talents, failures, delights. How could the all-encompassing great God be evident through puny me, through puny us? This comprises the mystery of the incarnation of the transcendent in the flesh. The chief contribution of depth psychology to theology lies in its making clear, again and again and again, that the flesh also includes the psyche.

There lives in us that which exceeds us, that we do not invent or control, and that we must descend from ego consciousness to meet. God also speaks through the psyche — our problems and inspirations, our dream images and conscious thoughts, our complexes and accomplishments, our impulses and confusions. We fear the psyche because it is more alive than we thought, not entirely under our command. If God also speaks to us through the psyche, that means that God speaks through all the parts of us and all the parts of the human community — including the shameful ones; the bad ones; the ones that are ill, weak, overly ambitious, grandiose; the relationships that hurt, that fail, not just the ones that fulfill; the neighborhoods that are rich as well as the ones that are poor. It means the whole thing, not just the good parts, the developed ones, our superior functioning. It means we can serve God even if mentally or physically ill. We can be a tax collector, a prostitute, and see the Holy, sometimes better than those who find so-called more honorable professions.

No one is excluded, because we all have a human psyche and because God reaches all of us there in the intimacies of our hearts and in the secrets of our communities. God comes to us in the prisons of our compulsions as well as the prisons of society, where we are naked, without defenses and bankrupt in our interior lives as well as in the poverty of our neighborhood.[19] If God also reaches us through the psyche, it

---

19. This inclusion of what Jung calls the shadow will be the subject of the second essay.

means we must wrestle with the astonishment, the fear, and even the panic at the gap between the images of the Holy that turn up in our dreams, our problems, our disputes with each other, our sexual congress, and those that occur in the representations for God in our traditional doctrine and ritual.[20]

A Third Kind of Knowing

Now, let us go into the kind of knowing that religious symbols initiate, especially when we experience their compelling, vibrant aliveness. Jung says of symbols that they express "something that is little known or completely unknown,"[21] describing "in the best possible way the dimly discerned nature of the spirit. A symbol does not define or explain; it points beyond itself to a meaning that is darkly divined yet still beyond our grasp, and cannot be adequately expressed in the familiar words of our language."[22] Symbols "are not objects of the mind, but categories of the imagination which we can formulate in ten thousand different ways. They are inexhaustible because they are before the mind, the basis of everything mental."[23] Hence, when we engage God through our traditional and personal images for God, we enter a zone of knowing, a style of consciousness that is itself paradoxical. The means of our knowing escort us into unknowing. In psychological language, we would describe it as a kind of knowing that lies between consciousness, where we are the subject and we have objects of knowing, and unconsciousness, where often we feel, as in the familiar dream of being chased by someone, that we are the object of an unknown subject.

Other scholars make the same point about religious symbols as pointers to a transcendent meaning which they cannot contain, thus holding

20. This will be the subject of the third essay.

21. Jung, *Symbols of Transformation,* p. 329.

22. Jung, "Spirit and Life," in *The Structure and Dynamics of the Psyche,* vol. 8 of *The Collected Works of C. G. Jung,* trans. R. F. C. Hull (New York: Pantheon, 1926/1960), para. 644.

23. Jung, *Dream Analysis,* ed. W. McGuire (Princeton: Princeton University Press, 1984), p. 330.

together the way of negation and the way of affirmation.[24] God transcends any pictures we make or find given to us; Jesus cannot be captured in any set of ethical rules or spiritual practices or rituals of worship that we ascribe to him. As Dorothy Emmet says, idolatry threatens the Protestant whenever we forget to deny the literal meaning of symbols.[25] Yet we need our pictures of God and our words for God, our human responses and constructions, what Paul Ricoeur calls the "manifestation in the sensible" because we are creatures of the senses. For him, the symbol possesses two vectors: one toward the linguistic or sensible expression of what is symbolized, and the other toward the intangible further reality that "both shows and hides itself."[26] Thus the ambivalence and ambiguity of religious symbolism is not, says Emmet, "the result of pious vagueness or of confusion of thought.... It is a precise way of conveying the fundamental dilemma of religious symbolism, which presents an analogue of the transcendent in the form of the phenomenal, of the infinite in the finite."[27]

Jung makes the same point about God's transcendence and our finitude more concretely and with more emotion. On the one hand, religious experience possesses a momentum that seems to demand its own expression, as if we could say God really does come to us and summon our response. Jung says our experience of God "strives for expression, and can be expressed only 'symbolically' because it transcends understanding. It *must* be expressed one way or another.... It wants to step over ... into visible life, to take concrete shape."[28] On the other hand, no form we give to God or to God in Christ can match the unoriginated, infinite God. We can only consent, or refuse. Jung says, "There is supreme submission. God can appear in any form he chooses.... To prescribe to that phenomenon which it ought to be, and not accept what it is, is not submission." And also, "The real Christ is the God of freedom."[29]

---

24. See Paul Ricoeur, *Freud and Philosophy,* trans. Denis Savage (New Haven: Yale University Press, 1970), p. 496.

25. Emmet, *The Nature of Metaphysical Thinking* (New York: Macmillan, 1957), p. 105.

26. Ricoeur, *Freud and Philosophy,* p. 7.

27. Emmet, *The Nature of Metaphysical Thinking,* p. 106.

28. Jung, *Letters,* vol. 1 (1973), January 10, 1929, p. 59 (italics in the original).

29. Jung, *Dream Analysis,* pp. 513, 519.

This attitude toward religious symbols as conveying God as transcending any form we can fashion applies directly to clinical practice and accents the peculiar Jungian approach to the psyche. We hear the patient's symptom and distress, and we have been trained and prepared through the mastery of theory, as well as through undergoing analysis of our own complexes, to bring a lot of knowledge to the therapeutic task. We know a great deal. Yet recognizing the objectivity of the psyche means that it is not all under conscious knowing and never will be, and that the more we go into ourselves, the more we come upon reality in its own right that transcends our whole psyche. Jung says the archetypes are "tools of God," a reality that speaks through the human psyche.[30] We know that we do not know what is being engineered for this person's destiny through this problem.

We must remain open to what purpose the symptom may be aiming at; at the same time, we want to know how to relieve the person of this symptom. Jung advises us to learn all we can, but when we face the living mystery of the person in our office, to throw out our theories; to listen, behold. Unknowing, not knowing, opening to the unknown, opening past our theory, waiting to hear, to catch in the patient's breathing, or flush of skin, or the odd dream image that something new is coming in — that must be our therapeutic endeavor. Near the end of his long and brilliant career, D. W. Winnicott said he bemoaned the harm he had done by speaking too soon, especially if his interpretations were correct, and that it could have amounted to a theft of soul from the patient.[31]

Opening to the unknown makes every analysis an adventure. We do not know where it will end up, but we do know that through the space in between knowing and not knowing, the path, the way for this particular analysand, will emerge. An example from clinical work turns on the tricky transference problem of the analysand questioning whether the analyst really cares for her. Therapeutic work is such an odd relationship, at once intimate and impersonal, full of exchange of feeling yet not lived outside the session, full of remarkable confidences, perhaps told to no one else in

---

30. Jung, *Letters*, vol. 2 (1975), October 1, 1953, p. 130.
31. Winnicott, *Playing and Reality* (London: Tavistock, 1971), p. 57.

one's entire life, yet one-way, not mutual. In asking whether or not the analyst cares for her, the analysand is asking about the place of this relationship in her personal life and in the large scheme of things. And inevitably, that question includes the analyst's failures to understand, the analyst's mistakes that always hurt the patient. Will you let me down? Will you be caring about me once the treatment is finished?

I have experienced more than once how an analysand resolves these questions, and the resolution turns on this new kind of knowing-unknowing. It is not so much anything I said in this instance, but rather my perspective in relation to the psyche — hers, mine, it. I marshal everything I know, and I let it go and open myself to what happens, what occurs to me, to the person, between us. We could call this a religious view; clinically we could call this a metapsychological position.

The example I select comes from a woman making her way into her inherited Jewish faith, though she went by way of Jesus. In this session she was talking about her Torah class. She reached the insight that all the commandments in Judaism are channels through which, in this physical, finite life here, we acknowledge the Oneness of things. All the specific items of the law are ways we link to the One, and hence are blessings. If we do not see these many prescriptions as links to the underlying unity of life, then they could be perverted into an obsessive-compulsive disorder. This is the law lived in the flesh to get to the deep meaning of the One behind everything. This connection has enabled this woman to overcome complex feelings of inferiority. She says, "If I participate, I have a contribution to make, to help God come into the world; in a sense, it is my job to take care of this You [God] and bring You into the world."

Her insight connects to the transference role I have played in her analysis and its resolution: she sees both of us connected to what I used to symbolize. Instead of going through me to this You, she sees both of us on the same side, so to speak, interested in this You that she finds in her study of Judaism. She says she feels I am now an inner presence, a witness to her work in analysis, and that she can finally set aside a lifelong conviction that she must earn the other's caring.

She says, "I do not have to do anything to earn or sustain your interest, to keep you interested in me, because you are already interested in this work going on in me, between the me and this You [God] in me. I, too, am interested in this larger It or You, in how it goes on in me. Your interest in me is already there, sort of impersonal — seeing how this relation between me and the You is operating — yet very personal because you care about how it unfolds in me, in my particular life."

This example illustrates the kind of knowing that emerges between our conscious and unconscious mental systems. Elsewhere I have called it double vision,[32] or simultaneous or synchronistic consciousness, because we are at once tuned into the words, mastery, and aim to communicate of consciousness — what Jung calls directed thinking — and the expressive, imagistic, instinct-backed process of the unconscious — what Jung calls nondirected thinking — which he rescued from being associated only with mental illness. Such nondirected thinking happens in all of us and is characteristic of children's mental processes, of creative people, and of dreaming.

The third kind of knowing partakes of both directed and nondirected thinking. In it we see as if with one eye on the here and now and the other eye on what my patient calls the One behind everything. In practice this means I am aware of thoughts that could be in response to what the analysand says, bits of pertinent theory that come to mind, and at the same time have a kind of open not-knowing where new images pop up — a dream the person had two years ago comes to mind, or one of my own memories, or a body sense. This empty attention is fertile and very different from the blankness that descends on me when another analysand in a rage devastates his own interior life and induces the same in me. There I cannot think, and nothing whatever occurs to me except the sense of having been stunned, as if under a spell where everything turns to deadness.

What happens in this third kind of consciousness in clinical work is a combination of our two mental systems of conscious and unconscious and of opposite things happening simultaneously. We are sure in this si-

---

32. Ulanov, *Spiritual Aspects of Clinical Work,* pp. 127-29. See also Ulanov, *The Unshuttered Heart: Opening to Aliveness/Deadness in the Self* (Nashville: Abingdon Press, 2007), chap. 2.

multaneous consciousness that the psyche is addressing us, that we do not invent the new that comes in; it confronts us, or hounds us, or summons us, and elaborates creatively on the events of our lives.

This necessary and health-giving work of the psyche is evidenced in the therapy Harry Wilmer did with Vietnam veterans suffering from post-traumatic stress disorder[33] and illustrated by my terminally ill patient in *The Wizards' Gate*. There death-dealing events flatten the person, and not until the psyche can start symbolically playing around with these events (for example, repetitious nightmares of the war trauma or the death-dealing tumor) can healing start. As the vet begins to dream not just the replay of the snipers killing all his buddies, but now maybe the scenario in which he is the sniper, or the scenario in which Harry is imported into the dream to survive the attack, the trauma begins to loosen its grip and mourning starts. With my patient, painting what faced her from the dark she was going into released her from the terror of her terminal diagnosis so that she could live right up until she died, and relate to her fate, thus turning it into destiny, if not providence.[34]

It is not all up to the psyche, however. Our acknowledgment — with our little ego the center of consciousness — must respond to what is happening. Those two things — the spontaneous activity of the psyche and our noticing it, along with the event that happened — make up the ingredients of healing therapeutic work. For example, when the vet tells his dream to Harry and to his fellow patients in the hospital in their dream circle, he attends to his telling; he responds to his experience of telling the dream to his comrades and his doctor. My patient responded in her efforts to paint and to both our responses to what she painted, a situation made all the more poignant because the tumor's placement had robbed her of words. We need to respond. We get a vote too, and can protest, argue, reject; or consent, agree gladly, speculate, ruminate; but respond we must. So this third kind of consciousness partakes of something that we do not originate and also of our personal rejoinder.

33. Wilmer, "War Nitemares: A Decade after Vietnam," in *Vietnam in Remission,* ed. James F. Veninga and Harry A. Wilmer (College Station: Texas A & M University Press, 1985).

34. Wilmer, "War Nitemares"; Ulanov, *The Wizards' Gate,* pp. 73-88.

In religious life, this third kind of consciousness is also present, I believe. There we get double vision, seeing our daily life and acknowledging in worship at the time of communion, for example, that the sacrifice of Christ is going on right now. The Eucharist we receive acts as a window onto eternity. Christ is knocking on our door right now as we rush to catch the subway or drive through traffic on the way to work. Right now, in the midst of whatever we are doing, Christ is offering the water of the spirit to drink. Both are true: finite and infinite, human and divine, simultaneous. To meditate on this theological fact is to build up combustion — sparks, flames!

Whether or not we define ourselves as religious in a denominational sense, Jung sees all of us as subject to this descent to the living psyche in each of us and among all of us. He sees us as religious animals, though not as pious as the wild ones whose instinct contains them within the will of God, doing what they are meant to do. Our religious instinct drives us to make meaning and create symbols to express it and our relation to it. Our religious instinct consists in the capacity to be consciously related to deity. Repressing or splitting away from this instinctual energy can make us fall ill just as surely as this happens in relation to our instincts of sex, or hunger, or aggression.[35] Just as denied sexuality can be displaced onto other objects, inflaming our attachment to them, so can our denied religious instinct. The energy of this instinct must go somewhere. If it is not directed to the ultimate, it will turn manic or make idols out of a finite good. Jung reminds us, "It is not a matter of indifference whether one calls something a 'mania' or a 'god.' . . . When the god is not acknowledged, ego mania develops and out of this mania comes sickness."[36]

---

35. Jung, *Psychology and Alchemy,* vol. 12 of *The Collected Works of C. G. Jung,* trans. R. F. C. Hull (New York: Pantheon, 1953), para. 11.

36. Jung, "Commentary on the Secret of the Golden Flower," para. 55; see also Ulanov, "Jung and Religion," in *Spirit in Jung* (Einsiedeln, Switzerland: Daimon, 1977/1999/2005), chap. 7.

Vocation

Jung was a psychiatrist. He did not set out to be a theologian, but was led into theological waters by the facts of the psyche. People did not get well, he discovered, until they rediscovered what life meant to them, and how to enter into the process of making and receiving this meaning.[37] The religious outlook was essential to health. To Jung, this was the call, vocation. Who are you meant to be? Have you avoided this? Have you consented to this? Nestled in this idea is the deeper one that to find self is to find God, and to find God is to find self (an Augustinian concept). They are not the same, but they are mysteriously linked.

When Jung talks of the objective psyche, he means we all share "the same primary psychic condition," just as we share the same human body structure. We have the same *kind of* psychic life, but not the same psychic life. We all share the potentials and problems having to do with sexuality, aggression, hunger, and dreaming, for example, yet individually and culturally we work out different responses and solutions. We can only speak of the objective psyche abstractly, "as a universal and uniform datum," but insofar as this objective psyche wants to live, to become actualized, it expresses itself in individual units, through individual human beings — in you, in me, in us. If we cannot bear the promptings of this urge toward individuation, then the objective psyche might seize us unconsciously, as an individual or as a group, and that always leads to catastrophe because then it "is not assimilated by any consciousness or assigned its place among the existing conditions of life."[38]

What Jung is after here, I believe, is the urge to individuate, to become all of whom we are given to be, as prompted by life itself: "The law of life always tends towards a life individually lived."[39] And this potential and burden belong to every human being, not to some elite who have analysis, not to some privileged who get religion, let alone to some sector defined by social, economic, or educational class, let alone by race or

37. Jung, *Memories, Dreams, Reflections,* p. 351.
38. Jung, *The Development of the Personality,* vol. 17 of *The Collected Works of C. G. Jung,* trans. R. F. C. Hull (New York: Pantheon, 1932/1954), para. 307.
39. Jung, *The Development of the Personality,* para. 307.

gender, but to each and every soul. This is the democracy of the psyche: the call, the vocation, to become all of whom you are given to be addresses itself to each and every one of us.[40]

How shall we respond? Response is required; it can be yes, no, fear, or release. Jung even sees neurosis as "a defence against the objective, inner activity of the psyche, or an attempt, somewhat dearly paid for, to escape [from] the inner voice and hence from the vocation."[41] We fear being called because we do not know by whom or to what. One of my analysands as a little girl had religious experiences, especially of Jesus, and had an answering rush of feeling and devotion, but also fear. In her little girl's mind, she only knew of missionary work as a religious vocation, and she feared leaving home for a strange land full of dirt and bugs. Thus even as a little child the theological question underlying her future life was cast: What will love of God ask me to sacrifice?

We fear this call because it will isolate us; people will say we are crazy, full of ourselves, caught up in a fantasy or a power trip and wanting to manipulate others. We will be alone, unpopular, outcast, and terrified of what may unfold if we say yes. Nonetheless, we each must answer, and, if yes, must give to this inner prompting the same trustful, observant, considering attitude we give to religious experience. Jung thus finds linked the call to be all of oneself and the call to God: "True personality is always a vocation and puts its trust in it as in God, despite its being . . . only a personal feeling."[42] "Fidelity to the law of one's own being is . . . a loyal perseverance and confident hope; in short, an attitude such as a religious man should have towards God."[43]

Lest we duck out by saying this is mere individualism, selfish indulgence, and grandiose self-idealization to the exclusion of our neighbor, we need only remember that we are all part of the people as a whole, and that each of us receives the same call. In this sense we are fellow refugees, sister sojourners. This is not our "own" law, but our response to the

---

40. Jung, *The Development of the Personality,* paras. 302, 307.
41. Jung, *The Development of the Personality,* para. 313.
42. Jung, *The Development of the Personality,* para. 300.
43. Jung, *The Development of the Personality,* para. 296.

necessity the psyche lays upon us and our struggle to find the means and forms to consent to it in the conditions of our individual lives.

Our personal response plays out in the conditions of our culture, our time in history, and our community, and may be our particular contribution to shared existence with others. To consent often means more suffering; to consent always means more consciousness of how much suffering there is among all of us. This is like the daughter who, among all the family members, seems to be the one to become conscious of the generational family complexes, as if the buck stops with her. She works out consciously in her individual way, in relation to family members, what they pass on to each other unconsciously. A child may be the abused victim who, as adult, does not pass on abuse to his own children, but instead works through the deep origins of such destructive behavior. Moreover, to take up one's own vocation means exposing oneself to what governs the objective psyche at this time in history, in the community, in the group, and sometimes even in the world, and suffering the problem in one's own individual life and working it over and over for its transformation.

Jung believed he did this and said he was "satisfied with the course my life has taken." Though he felt in himself a bundle of opposite responses — "distressed, depressed, rapturous . . . and incapable of determining ultimate worth or worthlessness . . . and no definite convictions" — he nonetheless said, "I feel a solidity underlying all existence and a continuity in my mode of being."[44] Let us hope we all feel such acceptance in looking over the arc of our lives.

From both psychological and theological perspectives, it is risky business to respond with all one's mind, heart, and strength to what summons us. As Jung puts it: "Surrender to God is a formidable adventure. . . . He who can risk himself wholly to it finds himself directly in the hands of God. . . . Christian faith insists on the deadly danger of the adventure."[45]

---

44. Jung, *Memories, Dreams, Reflections*, p. 358.

45. Jung, "Letter to Pere Lachat," in *The Symbolic Life*, vol. 18 of *The Collected Works of C. G. Jung*, trans. R. F. C. Hull (Princeton: Princeton University Press, 1954/1976), para. 178.

Where to Put the Bad?
Where to Put the Feminine?

Shadow and Ruthlessness

If we take seriously Jung's idea of the nature of our vocation to become all of ourselves, a call that feels like one issued from God, how do we respond? What happens when we pay careful, trustful attention to this prompting, this necessity to step forward from the shadows to become all of our being? Usually fear happens in us, for we think immediately of parts of us we do not want to include, parts that seem crazy or shameful. We think of parts of our neighbors and neighborhoods, of our world, that we do not want to venture toward, but prefer to keep "over there." Or we look at all these parts, our own or those of others, as problems to be solved, deficits to be fixed, faults to be reformed. We want to convert everyone to our point of view, to our vision of God, and even threaten ostracism if they do not comply.

The danger of this identification of our religious vision as the only true one — this casting out anyone who disagrees — we have seen up close, firsthand, recently, in the attacks of 9/11. "Those not identified with my version of Islam are," as an Imam said — explaining this view, which he identified as misguided, in a public forum in which we both participated — "infidel, dust." And indeed, in New York City, we still see remnants of the dust to which our neighbors were reduced, into which our buildings collapsed. The gigantic open space at Ground Zero reminds us of the huge hole created in the human family when we commit theological bullying: Believe as I do or you're dead, gone.

Fear, then, accompanies our vocation — the summons to a fuller, wider life — which for Jung is also one of greater consciousness. Fear participates in our project here of seeing the interweaving of the psyche as another means through which we refine theological positions. Specifically, fear of the bad jumps up, for where are we to put it? To admit the bad in ourselves, in our group, in our world — what Jung calls shadow contents (for usually it is the bad we leave in the shade while trying to illuminate the good) — we need ruthlessness. By this I mean an instinctive energy determined to see through to what is there and what is not there. Spontaneous, bounding, insistent, we experience an inner intensity to go at the emotional truth, the justice truth, the theological truth, to speak out about the elephant in the room of the faculty meeting. With gripping directness, and for the moment without concern for consequences to self or other, this ruthless energy goes after what is, not what should be, not what we need or wish or even fear to be, but what is. It takes a lot of energy to face the fact that I envy so-and-so; that I want to succeed and be on top; that I hold a grudge while denying I do; that I do not accept my body and do not want to, that I want another body; that I hate you for not seeing me, or loving me; that I have neglected my gifts. It takes ruthless energy to face the shadow. Yet vocation can begin through the shadow.

We often first hear the call through what appears to the ego as bad or different or other than what convention dictates, a convention to which we subscribe. A patient of mine found great relief in remembering why she had married her husband, a marriage that ended decades later in painful divorce. She had been berating herself for being so stupid to make such a bad choice. But her greater insight into her urgent need to get out of her original family, which was breaking her spirit, and in a culture that dictated that a girl could depart from her family only to marry, not just to be independent, brought her release from self-attack. She had not been so stupid; she had found the one available escape route. Other examples actually break rules that one may still hold dear. A man felt deep shock that he was engaged in an affair, saying, "It defies everything

I believe in; how could I be doing this?" Yet the thought of giving up this love made him feel that he would die; he had found some lost piece of soul he could not live without. Thus hoisted on his own cross, he suffered, being pulled apart in opposing directions.

More gripping still is the fact that the conflicts that rise up to confront us present not just our own parts of which we have been unconscious, but also those embedded in our community. The temptations of Christ give a striking example. Of course we want to feed starving babies, or bring peace to the world, or have one united faith among all peoples! How could we resist? The story of Jesus differentiating the one true thing that is first, the first thing before all other precious values, is truly astounding.

Jung goes so far as to say that the inner voice calling us to be all of ourselves usually sneaks in through something negative, making us conscious of evil as it afflicts everyone in our group, whether it be our neighborhood, our nation, or the whole human race.[1] But we experience it in our particular individual form, so we think that it is just our problem. Two dangers threaten. Because we may think this is only our shameful problem, we try to rid ourselves of it, which usually means projecting it onto our neighbor. We try to master it, fight it, banish it. Then we do not meet it and struggle with it until it transforms. The other danger is that we succumb entirely to it and go under. Neither changes the situation.

What does work change is to "succumb only in part" to shadow contents and to respond by asserting our ego values, and thus begin a strenuous, conscious dialogue between these coinciding opposites.[2] We suffer the conflict. We are stretched on cross-purposes and slowly assimilate something from both sides, from which a third new attitude, symbol, or possibility emerges as if like the voice of God.[3] From a psychological point of view, this process of what Jung calls the transcendent function[4]

---

1. Jung, *The Development of the Personality,* vol. 17 of *The Collected Works of C. G. Jung,* trans. R. F. C. Hull (New York: Pantheon, 1934/1954), para. 319.

2. Jung, *The Development of the Personality,* para. 319.

3. Ulanov, "Transference and the Transcendent Function and the Transcendence," chap. 13 of *Spiritual Aspects of Clinical Work* (Einsiedeln, Switzerland: Daimon, 2004), pp. 330-32.

4. Jung, "The Transcendent Function," in *The Structure and Dynamics of the Psyche,*

means differentiating the good and the bad mixed up in the prompting to individuation. Jung says, "The highest and the lowest, the best and the vilest, the truest and the most deceptive things are often blended together in the inner voice in the most baffling way, thus opening up in us an abyss of confusion, falsehood, and despair."[5] When individuals struggle to differentiate good and bad in themselves, their differentiation makes things clearer for the rest of us; the person doing it puts into the general psychic atmosphere possibilities of discernment not available to the rest of us before. In this way community builds up on a less-than-conscious level; it makes good more possible and evil more avoidable.

For example, in hindsight, if someone at Columbine High School had wrestled with the destructive energy expressed in kids casting out other kids as "the scum of the school," maybe the two boys would have been able to imaginatively conceive of ways other than murder and suicide to retaliate and assert their own value. Or, I remember, when my son was two and doing something destructive and dangerous, giving him a reasonable, even-toned lecturette on why this was wrong and not to be done. Nothing I said was bad; but my tone was contemptuous. I think I was worked up and mad and thought I must not take out my anger on my son, so I was reasonable instead. But the anger I did not face seeped through in a disrespectful tone, and he crumpled right before my eyes. I was horrified. Fortunately, I was also ineffective. Later, he did the same thing again and thus gave me another chance. Children are so generous. This time I faced my anger, which was at the boiling point. I didn't know what to do or say. So I just gave form to my anger. I dropped to the floor on all fours, his level, and roared. That certainly got his attention! Who is this tiger? He stopped whatever he was doing that was so bad and looked at me with curiosity. He did not crumple, and he did not repeat the dangerous behavior.

From a theological perspective, this facing the bad in us, without falling entirely under its spell and yet not fleeing upwards from it in zeal

---

vol. 8 of *The Collected Works of C. G. Jung,* trans. R. F. C. Hull (New York: Pantheon, 1916/ 1960), paras. 131-193.

5. Jung, *The Development of the Personality,* para. 319.

to fix it or eradicate it, means ruthlessly accepting all the way down that this bad trait or attitude or obdurate refusal — yes, that is me too, that is part of me. We never want to do this and have ready a string of "yes, but" reasons why this is not really true about us. But it is. In the parable of the sheep and the goats, Jesus says that insofar as you respond to the least person, you do it for me. He shows those who, to their surprise, turn out to be sheep, because they visited the person in prison, or brought the thirsty man water, or the naked woman clothes — that in fact they had brought these things to Jesus himself. We rightly apply this parable to our life with each other, to our concerns with social justice. But what about inner justice? What about the part of us imprisoned in rigid defenses or obsessive-compulsive disorder? Do we visit that part or scorn it? What about a vulnerability that is all but naked? Do we cover that defenselessness with caring? What about our soul that needs to be fed, to be reconnected to flowing feeling? Do we bring it any water, or just ignore it?

Theologically, to face the bad in us, the shadow, means to come face to face with the astounding fact that Paul announces: God loves us while we are yet sinners.[6] We do not have to be buffed up, healthy, analyzed, without problems. We are loved as we are — mixtures; stumblers; beggars; saying yes, no, I don't know to vocation; struggling. Jesus is born in the muck of the stable, not in the inn with reservations. Hence we dare not leave out the stable muck in our lives — marriage tensions, broken hearts, broken relationships, buried angers and grudge-holding, fraudulent acts, theft, meanness, refusal to try, hopes we will not acknowledge, mental confusion, social discrimination — these constitute the muck we know.

Clinically and in terms of practical living, Jung's notion of shadow is very useful, a real contribution to coming to terms with what we usually think we should exclude in both our individual and our social relations. On a personal level, our shadow is all we would not be, often all our parents told us was bad behavior; it is all we would improve, all we would fix and get over, move on from. It is all we dislike in this roommate for life.

6. Romans 5:8.

55

Our enemies can tell us what our shadow is in a minute, though it is hard for us to see because, like a physical shadow, it is always behind us, adding three dimensions, depth. Most of us have dreams of being chased by a shadowy figure; that was the origin of Jung's name for this complex. We find in our shadow complex what our ego deems negative, and usually it is. But we also may find in the shadow good parts, positive dreams, capacities for hope and creativity that we have left to languish. Sometimes it is the shadow part that saves our lives, that points the new direction.

As clinicians, we must face our shadow on a personal level in our clinical work, such as getting overly identified with our psychological theory and labeling our clients as if they were examples of different pathologies. Our theory, which can provide a helpful map to the unknown psychic terrain our clients are exploring, becomes then instead a weapon of contempt. It is hard to catch, because we are thinking or saying the right words, but our attitude is askew. We have lost touch with the mystery of this person right before us. Or, we must reckon with our own hate and how it comes into the analysis in which we are engaged.[7] We could say the same about our religious affiliation — that if we fall into identification with its doctrines and regulations and lose their precious symbolic function of pointing to the ultimate, then even our faith can become a weapon of attack against self and others, particularly our children.

On a cultural level, shadow means what our group, our tribe, our religion, our political party deems negative, out of bounds, to be shunned, to be improved, or to be punished. Behind every social oppression lurks a piece of group shadow whose members are exporting it onto others who are not of their tribe. When the shadow part is not faced, it goes unconscious and lives there. Like all unconscious contents, shadow parts fall into primary process mentation, a mental process that is called "primary" because chronologically it is our first mentation, and also because it is always there, operating in our unconscious until we die. In it everything mixes with everything else. Thus what I repress mixes with what you repress and amasses more energy, pressing for release into consciousness. Unguided by our personal ego consciousness and not chan-

7. Ulanov, *Spiritual Aspects of Clinical Work*, chap. 16.

neled through conscious cultural forms, these shadow affects and im-pulses can burst out in fits of rage, murderous attacks, sudden accidents. A man, for example, was angry with another man but never talked it over or faced the issue with him. He dreamt of taking the other man by the throat and bashing his head repeatedly against the floor. The bit of anger had swelled unconsciously to murderous intent.

Shadow parts are not pieces of information or mental concepts, but are alive, like animals in the basement. And these live contents, like trapped animals, want to get out into conscious life. If we do not face and work with these affects, they remain out of sight and out of reach of ego modification or reality testing, mixed with fantasy and unconscious in-stinctive energy, and they burgeon. If we do not acknowledge these af-fects, we project them onto neighboring groups with no actual reality contact to modify our demonizing of these others. The Serbians' view of the Croatians waxed to such an exaggerated pitch that it seemed to those in power justifiable to commit mass murder; genocide became their duty. And we could replicate these examples with those from the Croatians and other groups. The point is that without the intercession of consciousness,[8] the unconscious shadow bits pressing for consciousness get projected and acted out on our neighbors in prejudice, discrimina-tion, and even persecution and genocide.

Even more frightening is the archetypal level of shadow that ad-dresses whatever we define as evil per se, evil in itself, underlying all epi-sodes of bad behavior. Christians might call up the symbol of the devil; or we might conceptualize evil as humans' inhumanity to humans; or we might hypothesize a principle of evil as belonging to being. Whatever we name as evil, it points to a mysterious nullity that infiltrates all our re-solves to do better. We do not do what we wish to do, and should; we do what we do not wish to do and should not do.

For example, on a personal level, after fighting with someone we love, we know if we just say, "I was a fool — I'm sorry," that would go a long way to heal the hurt and mend the rift, but we do not say it! Why

---

8. Ann and Barry Ulanov, *Religion and the Unconscious* (Louisville: Westminster/John Knox Press, 1975), chap. 11.

not? Who knows?! Similarly, on a social level, full of anger at injustice played out on our group, we know the Christian counsel to pray for our enemies. But we want revenge, payback. Why? Who knows? At best we may be able to eke out a prayer between clenched teeth. Jung helps us see that that is probably the best course because we consent to suffer the cross-purposes of the outrage and deep hurt the injustice inflicts, and of the hope to utter such a prayer. We do not hop over the anger but suffer it. If we hop over anger, that means that we repress the anger again into the common pool that contaminates our neighbors' well and fuels more injustice.

Even worse, on an archetypal level, the great trick of the devil is to convince us that he does not exist,[9] that we are being overly dramatic, even hysterical, to feel such menace threatening us. But the devil is known to be a fraud, a liar, a cheat, and a scam artist, promising everything and delivering nothing. Here we meet shadow that is beyond our personal limits and abilities to face and integrate.

At the personal level we can assimilate some of our shadow, and this is to everyone's benefit, including our own. We respond to all of our feelings and intents and do not just export them to our neighbor's lawn, or to our children. We grow in depth, with the shadow backing us up; we become three-dimensional, and we cease to pollute the atmosphere. On the cultural level, we can assimilate some degree of our group shadow-projection. The great thing about America's democracy is that we can object, protest, and not be killed or imprisoned. We have built some degree of shadow recognition and negotiation into our political system. But on the archetypal level, facing evil is like facing a tidal wave. Our puny selves are no match. Only Jesus was called into the desert for a face-to-face confrontation with the shadow side of the reigning values of his culture — to feed the hungry, to unite the governments, to recognize one God. In the face of evil itself, finally, we must depend on what transcends us.

9. Ulanov, *Picturing God* (Einsiedeln, Switzerland: Daimon, 1986/2002), pp. 127-28; and Ulanov, *The Wisdom of the Psyche* (Einsiedeln, Switzerland: Daimon, 1988/2000), pp. 33-35.

Shadow and Dependence

Here we enter deep waters, for dependence is part of the muck of our stable too. We fear dependence and try to master and control our lives, our children, our nation, even our God, forgetting that God, like a tiger, always jumps out of any cage of doctrine or rules we construct. Or we may indulge dependence by casting authority onto those we make into parental surrogates — the church, the nation, the neighbors' standards, the spouse's views, the parent now dead. We fear to take the burden onto ourselves to see what is there and not there, what we think, what we do to solve the conflict of our love and hate, whom we would put in the White House as president. We fear the weight of responding to all our human feelings, and instead parcel them out and try to remain good girls and boys, doing what we are told.

Jung remains a paradoxical figure here, helpful in making us face our own authority as well as the dependence our faith summons from us, while he himself says he does not bow all the way to the ground. Like Barth, Jung puts himself under transcendent authority that must be obeyed. Jung's image for this authority is the Self, his God-image, and he describes the experience in this way: "The psyche, an objective fact, hard as granite and heavy as lead, confronts a man as an inner experience and addresses him in an audible voice, saying, 'This is what will and must be.'"[10] "There is supreme submission."[11] We must consent to depend on the unknown "transcendental Thou."[12]

Yet Jung also objects to too much dependence, to shoving all our problems onto God, saying "God's will be done" while in fact refusing to take up our cross ourselves.[13] This childish evasion of growing up to the harshness of reality and the fact of the unconscious shadow amounts to

---

10. Jung, *The Development of the Personality,* para. 303.

11. Jung, *Dream Analysis,* ed. William McGuire (Princeton: Princeton University Press, 1984), p. 513.

12. Jung, *Letters,* 2 vols., ed. G. Adler and A. Jaffé, trans. R. F. C. Hull (Princeton: Princeton University Press, 1973), vol. 1, September 10, 1943, p. 338.

13. Jung, "Jung and Religious Belief," in *The Symbolic Life,* vol. 18 of *The Collected Works of C. G. Jung,* trans. R. F. C. Hull (Princeton: Princeton University Press, 1976), para. 1661.

using religion as a defense, much as Freud criticized. Even with his own God-image of the Self, Jung remains ambivalent. He tells of a dream in which his father would take him up to the "highest presence" ascending from a mandala-like structure of a large hall. Before ascending the stairs, his father "knelt down and touched his forehead to the floor." Jung says, "I imitated him, likewise kneeling, with great emotion. For some reason I could not bring my forehead quite down to the floor — there was perhaps a millimeter to spare." He reflects, "I had to submit to this fate, and ought really to have touched my forehead to the floor, so that my submission would be complete. But something prevented me from doing so entirely, and kept me just a millimeter away. Something in me was saying, 'All very well, but not entirely.' Something in me was defiant and determined not to be a dumb fish; and if there were not something of the sort in free men . . . where would be his freedom? And what would be the use of that freedom if it could not threaten Him who threatens it?"[14]

It is out of this ambivalence that Jung wrote his meditation on Job and eventually crafted his own devotion to God. In sum: For Jung, we serve God by becoming conscious of the polarities of existence in ourselves and in being itself. In answer to the earlier question of where to put the bad, Jung puts it in God. Evil is a principle of existence, of being itself. Job's protest about the suffering of the innocent occasions Yahweh to become conscious of the vying of good and evil in the Godhead, of the shadow in himself. Christ answers Job's protest by taking on himself the sins of the world, submitting to the fate of the innocent sufferer. Christ bequeaths to us the Spirit that goes on incarnating in us, which means that we accept conscious suffering of good and evil in our own conflicts and in our world. By struggling to integrate the opposites, we incarnate God's struggle; we too carry the cross.[15] Jung writes, "The whole man is challenged and enters the fray with his total reality. Only then can he become whole and only then can 'God be born,' that is, enter into human reality . . ."; "the myth of the necessary incarnation of God — the essence of the

---

14. Jung, *Memories, Dreams, Reflections,* ed. Aniela Jaffé, trans. Richard and Clara Winston (New York: Pantheon, 1963), p. 219.

15. Ulanov, *Spirit in Jung* (Einsiedeln, Switzerland: Daimon, 1999/2005), p. 135.

Christian message — can then be understood as [our] creative confrontation with the opposites and their synthesis in the self, the wholeness of [our] personality . . . as the *coniunctio oppositorum* . . . or as the *unio mystica.* In the experience of the self it is no longer the opposite 'God' and ['human'] that are reconciled . . . but rather the opposites within the God-image itself. That is the meaning of divine service, of the service which [we] can render to God, that light may emerge from the darkness. . . ."[16]

We can respect Jung's long arriving — indeed, over the span of his whole life — at a clarity of how he is devoted to God. We can benefit from his insisting that we face our shadows and not pile them onto each other or onto God. We can applaud his faithfulness to human freedom, that even in the face of the "ultimate presence," that tiny spark must not be extinguished, lest there be no fire in the world, no human creativity, no mutuality of loving between human and divine.

We are familiar with Jung's belief that images for the Self, which are indistinguishable from God-images, contain good and evil. The Self is an archetype, the navel that centers the archetypal world of the objective psyche. Like all archetypes, the Self has two opposite poles, negative and positive; good and evil reside in the Self. At the archetypal level, Jung is right, I believe. Good and evil contend with each other as opposites. This is a tragic view of reality, that evil and good are principles of being itself, constantly in strife. All archetypes are bivalent. It is at the archetypal level that Jung's good-and-bad God dwells.

Here the Christian tradition, as I understand it, takes a different direction. I see Self-images not as God but as bridges to the reality that transcends the whole psyche. The Self archetype links to what is beyond the archetypal layer, to reality itself, which authors us. The Self is that in us that knows about God. Christian tradition also recognizes the fact that evil and good vie in this world for victory, never subduing nor being defeated by each other. In the words of John's Gospel, good is like light shining in darkness, never understood and never conquered.[17] But nei-

16. Jung, *Memories, Dreams, Reflections,* pp. 337, 338.

17. S. L. Frank, *The Light that Shineth in Darkness,* trans. Boris Jakim (Athens: Ohio University Press, 1989), p. 126.

ther does the light outshine the darkness; it never wins in unambiguous fashion.

At the ego level, both personally and culturally, we experience the bivalent archetypal field as good and evil struggling with each other, neither fully victorious nor vanquished. Light comes into the world, and the darkness does not comprehend it. If we use blackness as the symbol of the transcendent, we can equally well say that the gleaming blackness in which the Holy dwells is not understood or received by the glaring, parching light. At the level of ego consciousness, these two always contend. But at the depth level, the Christian faith proclaims, light has already conquered; we have already been brought home to the cooling depth of darkness. God has come and entered our long day's dying, our being dust, and to dust we return; God has taken up into God's self the suffering that human life entails, which we magnify by inflicting it upon each other. God has taken responsibility for creating us free creatures who can refuse God, taking the consequences onto the cross, where the innocent Holy One suffers as if guilty. The logic of evil stops here.

Another way to describe this same point is to see that on the ego level, each of us is like a blip on a radar screen, inconsequential in the large scheme of things. At the depth level of reality, the reality that transcends the whole psyche to which Self and God-images make a bridge, each of us is known, cherished, irreplaceable. We know this by faith; it is unverifiable by the senses, and surpasses logic. It is gift, and gifts can only be refused or received. Here, in contrast to Jung, our dependence is complete. The gift is given by grace, and arrives through grace, and grace empowers us to receive it. We choose to submit, freely, and hence our freedom is affirmed, not extinguished.

On a smaller level, though felt as momentous if we experience this mystery in which divine mingles with human in the gift of salvation, is the experience of forgiveness. To say that we forgive, when in fact we hop over our fury, our deep hurt, never works. Blood seeps out from the wound that we neglect. That is to ignore the shadow. To enter the fury of our wound is consciously to suffer rage and pain. Some hurts are so big that the suffering seems to go on forever. These are the hurts that bring people to us as clinicians. How does one get over childhood abuse, sexual molestation, murderous affect, rejection, loss, neglect? In addition, some of us get caught in historical wounds so great that they make a huge hole in the fabric of the human family. How do we span a holocaust, a forced starvation, a sniper shooting, a building bombing, a 9/11? We do our work; we process our rage and grief; we bleed our life's blood. It may be a personal hurt of one friend betraying another that adds shame to the original wound. We feel ashamed to hurt so much when we compare our suffering to what people suffer in war — terror, rape in camps, loss of home, of loved ones. But we do hurt. We cannot heal; we cannot transform this suffering.

Here the Christian tradition offers a kind of dependence that does not hop over working on our own shadow stuff, our own struggle with the opposites. We can confide our suffering in Christ; we can bring it to this God-man hanging on the cross. One woman saw herself as putting her hurt right into the wound in Christ's side. She went as far as she could with processing this material in analysis, and then she depended utterly on asking for Christ's help, her forehead all the way to the ground, her wound held in his. From time to time, she would take the complex of rage and hurt out again from Christ's side. Imaginatively, she would see her wound as still festering and infected, but better around the edges. Then she would confide it again into Christ's wound. And so on, until, to her amazement, like a wind blowing from she knew not where, a forgiveness flowed into and through her, releasing her from shame at being so woundable, relieving her from guilt at the rage she felt toward the one who so hurt her, setting her free toward this other person. It was done, forgiven.

The basic dividing in the road between Jung and Christian tradition articulates itself in different understandings of the traditional notion of evil as *privatio boni,* as the deprivation of good. We can feel indebted to Jung for resisting the attempt to reduce evil to what goes wrong with our parents and how they treated us, remembering that they too were children of former parents, and all the way back to Adam and Eve. In addition, Jung presses us not to fall for easy answers to the mystery of evil, and to face on the practical level how to integrate and not project the bad in us onto others and into the collective shared atmosphere. Hence depth psychology spades up shadow stuff — anger, destructiveness, punitive guilt-making, and the inevitability of the negative. The Christian tradition includes the necessity of confession, which means facing our shadow and, further, the transforming of generalized evil into specific acts of sin — that is, a breaking of relationship to the source, to the author, to the originating God.

Christian tradition asserts that it is as if God says, "Yes, I take responsibility for creating you as free creatures who can choose to refuse me. I climb on the cross and become there not just the God who unconditionally loves you and forgives and accepts you, but also the God who takes your worst. I suffer the consequences of your sin, just as does the innocent bystander." Walter Lowe thinks that God's forbidding our eating from the Tree of Life is not so much an interdiction as it is a creative limit.[18] In psychological jargon we would call it a frame, a container for innocence and freedom that allows human and divine to co-exist and not cancel each other. Confession, when done freely from the heart, clears a space like that of innocence again where God's freedom and ours meet. We turn and are turned again to live from the source, the origin point we symbolize with our pictures for God.

For Jung the *privatio boni* means that evil does not exist with the same force as does good — and therefore we can get round it, because it is insubstantial. Thus we can deny our shadow because it is not really real. I disagree; I find the *privatio boni* a sophisticated idea, both psychologically and theologically. Evil does exist as an existential force, real, effective, but it does not exist as does good. It exists as making absence where there is presence; as a howling mood of resentment, unbudging in the face of anyone's attempt to reach us; as a refusal to recognize the presence of this person in front of us as a person. It demotes; subtracts; abstracts; chooses void over substance, goneness over being here, now, facing the task. We all know the dangerous passage in successful clinical work where the person is no longer caught by an addiction or compulsion or despondent depression. Now there is a tiny but clear bit of elbow

18. Lowe, *Innocence and Experience: A Theological Exploration: Evil, Self, and Culture,* ed. Marie Coleman Nelson and Michael Eigen (New York: Human Sciences Press, 1984), pp. 260ff.

room. They see it, know alternatives, can fight it, can choose otherwise. At this moment every clinician is completely dependent on his or her clients: which way will they choose? We cannot choose for them, but only wait in hope.

Related to this issue of evil as the sin of turning away from primary relationship, from the center of all life, and the refusal to exercise that tiny bit of elbow room, is Jung's notion of God, not as *summum bonum* but, as I said earlier, the bundle of opposites, the *complexio oppositorum,* that needs our devoted service in struggling to transform them into a wholeness both in ourselves and in God. Such struggle amounts to our contribution toward God becoming the conjunction of opposites, the *coniunctio oppositorum.*

For Christians, God is good, not a mixture of good and evil.[19] Here is a picture of a God who enters into human suffering, who in Christ takes on himself the agonies, sorrows, and griefs of humans overcome by sin and captured by the principalities and powers of evil. What the Son suffers, the Father suffers, for they are of the same substance. So the heart of reality abides in our hearts so afflicted by suffering. God's engagement with us in our worst captivity is an act of choice, moved by compassion. We who are captives cannot see the graciousness of God, but picture God as punitive, distant, impassible, vengeful. What distinguishes God from us is precisely this compassion to take into the Godhead the worst we can do, and to still abide with us and for us. The creative limit, which, as Paul Ricoeur says, "does not repress, but orients and guards freedom,"[20] we see only as prohibition or empty alternative.

In Jesus we see the alternative of choosing the Tree of Life fulfilled. Evil does not go away. Indeed, it afflicts him from his birth in poverty and filth, to his parents' flight for his life when he was just a few days old, to his being the catalyst for massacre of other infants, and on and on into the mounting of the cross, that other tree that reveals an abyss of love that is stronger than the abyss of death. I like Lady Julian's words that

19. See Ulanov, *The Wisdom of the Psyche,* chap. 2.
20. Ricoeur, *The Symbolism of Evil* (New York: Harper & Row, 1967), p. 250; cited in Lowe, *Innocence and Experience,* p. 261.

sum up how to see good and evil and God. She says, "God authors all good and suffers all evil."[21]

The Feminine

Lady Julian's words sound the presence of the feminine approach to these mysteries. The feminine mode of being, just like the masculine, belongs to all of us. It is a style of thinking and doing, experiencing and acting, that is characterized by going down into what happens, into the matter of things and what matters. It is to live with the opposites, their division and their mingling. Its style of perception issues upwards from body instinct and impulse, unconscious affect and spontaneous image; it issues in hunch, in dream image, in the amazing linking of heretofore separate things. We need this style of perceiving and connecting in this our new century, with its many divisions in communities across the world.

Jung wrestles with the image for God of the Trinity, quite rightly asking for all of us, Where is the feminine? His solution adds Mary to the Trinity[22] as the Spirit or as the fourth member. To me this is an intellectual solution, a sort of overdone masculine fix-it approach, to stick in the missing element; but it does not include the brooding pondering of the heart that issues in living it in the flesh.[23] I pay close attention to the image itself and its entry into the world through Mary. She houses the Word sent by God, in which God lives, who will leave us the Comforter, the consoling and igniting Spirit. She houses in human flesh the Trinity that houses her.

Are we then, all of us — men and women alike — are we the missing feminine, the fourth that embodies the mystery of the three, the earth in

21. Julian of Norwich, *Showings,* trans. Edmund Colledge, O.S.A., and James Walsh, S.J. (New York: Paulist Press, 1978), p. 199.

22. Jung, *Psychology and Religion: West and East,* vol. 11 of *The Collected Works of C. G. Jung,* trans. R. F. C. Hull (New York: Pantheon, 1938/1958), paras. 98-107; and Jung, "A Psychological Approach to the Dogma of the Trinity," in *Psychology and Religion: West and East,* paras. 240-295.

23. Ulanov, *The Wisdom of the Psyche,* p. 96.

whom God plants his coming into humanity? Is the feminine mode of being in us the house for the birth of the divine into the world of individual persons and communities? The feminine mode is the process wherein we be and become. The endlessly circulating love in God takes up residence in the human, pulling us into its currents.[24] What does that mean practically? It means, for now, in these decades, that the Holy comes into us through the feminine mode of being in each of us, moving us to live this love into the world.

In previous centuries the masculine mode of being gave access to these mysteries. We abstracted upwards from the tumult of instinctive life and found refuge in the Trinity as the unchanging eternal, or the ever rational, the pure, removed from the mess of human instincts and conflicts. But in the last decades of theology, where the direction has been to bring God down into human realities of race, politics, and gender, what opens us to receive this divine offering is the feminine mode of being. Nothing is in the abstract; all is in the flesh, symbolized by Jesus being born from Mary's womb. For what we seek is not a solution to evil but a conjunction, an inhabiting of God's house.

A startling example of this approach is given by a young woman who embodies, in her response to the crushing evil of the Holocaust, not a theory, but the fact of her own livingness in the face of destruction. Etty Hillesum was a young Jewish Dutch woman living in Amsterdam during the time the Nazis were taking over that city. As a member of the Jewish Council, she was accorded a certain freedom to come and go from the deportation camp from which Jews were shipped off to die in Auschwitz. So she suffered the increasing restrictions imposed on Jews in Amsterdam: they were evicted from their homes, prohibited from using the city parks, restricted to designated out-of-the-way stores to buy food. More and more laws, and less and less freedom. Finally, she too became an inmate of the deportation camp, as were her father, mother, and brother.

---

24. Ulanov, *The Wisdom of the Psyche,* pp. 97-98. For discussion of feminine and masculine modes of being, see Ulanov, *The Feminine in Jungian Psychology and in Christian Theology* (Evanston, Ill.: Northwestern University Press, 1971), chap. 9; and Ulanov, *Receiving Woman: Studies in the Psychology and Theology of the Feminine* (Philadelphia: Westminster, 1981), chap. 4.

She refused to escape, choosing instead to devote herself unreservedly to the service of others in the camp — helping with screaming babies, frightened children, exhausted mothers. Eventually, she herself was shipped off to death.

She writes in her letters and diaries, which faced a terrific struggle to get published: "God is not accountable to us for the senseless harm we cause one another. We are accountable to Him!" "I have looked our destruction, our miserable end which has already begun in so many small ways in our daily life, straight in the eye and accepted it into my life, and my love of life has not been diminished." "And that part of our common destiny which I must shoulder myself, I strap tightly and firmly to my back; it becomes a part of me. . . ."[25]

In Jung's words, she held the opposites — faced her own shadow and the dreadful shadow that darkened all of her continent. In the midst of terror that grew ever greater, so that she said "the surface of the earth is turning into a concentration camp," she also would write, "At night the barracks sometimes lay in the moonlight, made out of silver and eternity: like a plaything that has slipped from God's preoccupied hand. . . ." In this hell she wrote again and again, "Despite everything, life is full of beauty and meaning."[26] In theological terms, she faced evil, and it did not destroy the good. The abyss of love did prove stronger than the abyss of death.

25. Hillesum, *Letters from Westerbork,* trans. Arnold J. Pomerans (New York: Pantheon, 1986), pp. 127, 131, 147.

26. Hillesum, *Letters from Westerbork,* pp. ix, xi.

God-Images and the Life of Faith

In the church service of Holy Communion, after the receiving of the Eucharist, a prayer of thanks is offered. In my tradition, the prayer begins, "Almighty and everliving God. . . ." "Living" means animate, in the body, alive, quick, in the flesh, existing, incarnate, persisting, prevailing, subsisting, drawing breath. Whether from a conversion or gradual growth, faith, to be alive, constantly renews itself as a living relationship with the living God. Yet what is living here on earth is in the body, both individual and corporate. Body is definite form, boundaried, limited into this particular manifestation of life. This relationship with God, then, is at once spirited, expansive, boundless, and also concrete, specific, in the flesh. Jung says, "The feeling for the infinite . . . can be attained only if we are bounded to the utmost . . . in the experience: 'I am only that!' . . . In such awareness, we experience ourselves concurrently as limited and eternal, as both the one and the other. In knowing ourselves to be unique in our personal combination — that is, ultimately limited — we possess also the capacity for becoming conscious of the infinite. But only then!"[1]

How then do we unfold in relation to the living God giving us food from the heart of reality, ushering us into holy mysteries and the mystical body of Christ? How does this process get initiated? And what does

---

1. Jung, *Memories, Dreams, Reflections*, ed. Aniela Jaffé, trans. Richard and Clara Winston (New York: Pantheon, 1963), p. 325.

depth psychology contribute to it? Jung says, without qualification, that whatever we experience, we do so through the psyche, which is itself alive and which includes the unconscious. The unconscious communicates through the body, both individually and corporately, through affect-laden images that picture instincts, the thrumming of the mysterious gift of life itself. Those of you who minister to persons who are dying know the presence of this thrumming and its distinct, immediate absence when the person dies. It is as if they were here and now they are not. Their spirit may hover near, but they are gone.

I use the word "image" to refer to the great range of ways we differently apprehend God: some of us visually, others of us through body sensations, textures, smells, sounds; through nearness or distance. The ways we conduct our spiritual journey, and the ways it conducts us into greater intimacy with God, operate in the space between the subjective images we have for God and the objective ones we receive from our religious tradition, and in the space between all our human images for the Holy and the Holy itself, which breaks every image because nothing we construct can harness the infinitely free God. I have written elsewhere about this space,[2] drawing out the religious implications of D. W. Winnicott's term "transitional," but we could also call this space imaginal, that of the imagination, which is not a threat to faith, but its servant. How can the mental processes of the tiny ant threaten the giant elephant? How can the small human grasp the infinite God?

We have pictures that rise up in us autonomously, spontaneously because that is the psyche's language, and we receive pictures fashioned by centuries of other human psyches, canonized in Scripture and in worshipping traditions. Nonetheless, when we want to relate to all these pictures, doctrines, rituals, and Scripture passages, we still conjugate the space between them and us through images or their imaginative equivalents. We make these gifts real to us in our daily living by this process of translation; and we are translated into these Holy mysteries by these gifts of tradition pulling us in directions and into possibilities we could

---

2. Ulanov, *Finding Space: Winnicott, God, and Psychic Reality* (Louisville: Westminster/John Knox Press, 2001), p. 18.

not invent for ourselves. Otherwise, though we may recite traditional prayers or creeds or Scripture, their life does not bloom in us, does not scatter seeds of new life. Instead, we settle for religion by rote, or obedient compliance, not beholding the saying attributed to Jesus: "Those who are near to me are near to the fire."[3]

The Living God

For a living faith — one that goes on growing, generating compassionate actions in the world, begetting little epiphanies that mirror the gift of God's self-disclosure in Christ; one that is not stuck in the original conversion event, so that we repeat it compulsively and fear to change anything lest we lose it — we must engage in constant conversation with God, who is a living God. Our living psyche meets the living God; the living God meets our living psyche.

A conversation generates back and forth between the structured forms of our tradition and personal images that emerge in spontaneous living and praying, and each engenders the other. Because of personal experience of Jesus, we may move from traditional images of him as teacher and prophet to an image of him as priest, or even bridegroom. Or, the other way around: the traditional image of Jesus as Son may open to us the profound depth of God as Father, not a principle of being, now not even source, but a personal, relating heart of reality that cherishes us as daughters and sons. We feed the traditions of dogma by making them real through our idiosyncratic images of God; tradition feeds us by bringing to us what countless minds and prayers have turned over and refined, which exceeds what our limited perceptions can achieve. Like little trickles of water, or even a small stream, we feed the great tributaries of tradition that run to the wide-open sea. And it, the sea itself, runs into our little brooks and byways of water, supporting them with its largeness and often changing their course. Back and forth, we contribute to the liv-

3. Cited in Jung, *Symbols of Transformation,* vol. 5 of *The Collected Works of C. G. Jung,* trans. R. F. C. Hull (Princeton: Princeton University Press, 1912/1967), para. 245.

ingness of faith, and its treasure-house of imagery feeds our own particular journey.

Startling as it may sound, we can see the truth of John Ashton's assumption in his William James Lecture at Harvard, that "any plausible explanation of the origins of Christianity is . . . one focused upon the mystical experiences of Jesus . . . at the moment of his Baptism and of his Temptations in the desert. . . ."[4] Jesus' mystical experience reveals him as God's Son, forming his personal image of God as Father: the center of reality reveals itself as a Father speaking to his beloved Son. So potent was his mystical event, so quickening was the Spirit with which it descended upon Jesus, that it has shaped generations of believers to this day. Ashton says of Jesus, "He heard God addressing him as a son. The prophetic essence of what he heard can be summed up as the fatherhood of God . . . [and] Jesus saw the spirit descending upon him like a dove . . . [bestowing] an overwhelming sense of the presence of the spirit."[5]

We too must bring to consciousness the God-images that form within us and reckon with their shaping power. Here we circle back to my remarks in the first essay, that Christians fear to do this. Perhaps some of us now feel this fear of the psyche, that there lives in us that which exceeds us, that we do not invent or control, that talks to us, reaches out to grab us, comes over us, and that we must descend from ego consciousness to meet. This is the living psyche, and especially its unconscious processes that go on in us from birth to death. God speaks to us through the psyche and through the unconscious just as much as God speaks to us through events in the world, through other people, and through worship. God speaks to us through Scripture, through direct mystical or conversion experience. To relate to these momentous events, we must process the living God through the living psyche.

For us to withstand the living God, to live an alive faith, we must include — in our prayers as well as our actions — the living psyche, both conscious and unconscious. The psyche speaks to us in images, or their

4. Ashton, "The Religious Experience of Jesus," *Harvard Divinity Bulletin* 32 (Fall/Winter 2003): 17.

5. Ashton, *The Religious Experience of Jesus,* p. 18.

equivalent representations of the other senses — fragrance, sound, touch, taste. Theologically, this fact of the living psyche conceptualizes itself in the *imago dei*. We are created in the image of God; the mysterious, creative power and presence at the heart of life so exceeds our grasp that we are driven to use symbolic pictures and actions to escort us into its presence. Yet this creative creativity also exists in us. We too know a spark of this igniting fire deep inside us, flashing between us, as the desire to create — an attitude, a connection, a prayer, a poem, a relationship, a work of art, a business, a new recipe or pattern, whether for a jacket or a scientific experiment. We too possess, each and every one of us, a capacity to make something of our experience, of what happens to us, even the trauma that befalls us. This fact provides the ontology that underlies the faith that makes therapy with the psyche possible. We believe something can happen if we relate to what has happened; we can rescue past into present to unfold into a wider, more free future.

This is not theory that I am propounding. The unconscious is a fact. Any psychology, any theology must take it into account. Jung proposes a method to do just that. Distinct from all other analytical schools, his school of thought leaves a legacy to patients that allows it to be done with analysis and the analyst. What Jung calls the transcendent function is an effective means to collaborate with our religious instinct.

The Transcendent Function

The transcendent function is a natural process where opposite attitudes or goals or impulses — complex bundles of image, affect, instinct — coincide and conflict. We feel tossed from one to the other, much like a tennis ball in an intense match. Or, more often, we side with one opposite — thinking it is the right one to follow, the reasonable one — only to be upended by the other opposite seizing us. What are examples? Everything from knowing about the correct diet to follow while being seized by a hunger attack and gobbling chocolate chip cookies (one woman analysand says that that is the archetypal cookie), to getting distinct hunches that my orientation, my whole way of proceeding, is changing, such as in retirement, and yet resisting it for dear life. Such conflicts of opposites may be everything from knowing I should have a schedule and finding myself always procrastinating, to feeling the transcendent beckoning and rigidly grasping reason to resist it.

Jung gives an example of a patient who suffered from the delusion that he had cancer, when countless doctors assured him he did not. Jung took his conviction seriously, that it was as if something alien was growing in the patient against his will and he must attend to it or it would kill him. Resisting the savior impulse, Jung did not claim to know what this was and told his patient, "Look at your dreams; see what the psyche says." The dreams pictured the dreamer in churches and warned him that he could not use religion as an escape from engaging this other, a woman, who addressed him.[6] Thus the dreamer embarked on a path that slowly came into view as he responded to his dreams.

The Self, if resisted, demands the sacrifice of ego. We feel it as defeat, going through the fire, descending into the abyss, or simply the unraveling of our known way of living. Cooperating with this dynamism feels like groping in the dark, with only a scintilla of light to guide us; yet we feel an authoritative presence we must obey. A nun went through this fire just after she renewed her vows at her jubilee quarter-of-a-century celebration of her initial vows. Everything she thought she knew about God met only darkness, an end. Yet, she said, I must go on praying, though my old prayers do not work anymore. It is like waiting for the important phone call, so you don't want to be out when it comes.[7]

Jung found that the psyche naturally goes back and forth between the opposites and slowly builds up a third alternative that includes both sides but also something new. That is what he means by transcendent. Something builds up, transcending the conflict, and functions to resolve

6. Jung, *Psychology and Religion: West and East,* vol. 11 of *The Collected Works of C. G. Jung,* trans. R. F. C. Hull (New York: Pantheon, 1938/1958), paras. 12-21; Jung, *Psychology and Alchemy,* vol. 12 of *The Collected Works of C. G. Jung,* trans. R. F. C. Hull (New York: Pantheon, 1953), para. 293. For extended examples, see Ulanov, *The Functioning Transcendent* (Wilmette, Ill.: Chiron, 1996), chaps. 3, 5, 9, and 10.

7. Ulanov, "The Holding Self: Jung and the Desire for Being," in *Spirit in Jung* (Einsiedeln, Switzerland: Daimon, 1992/1999/2005), pp. 70-74.

it. The unconscious autonomously throws up images, and consciously we must receive and wrestle with them. If we do not, the images recede and others come up. The sad plight of our neighbors confined to mental hospitals illustrates the necessity of conscious engagement. Otherwise, like the waves, the unconscious rises and falls and nothing happens, nothing changes. Conscious participation is essential but not sufficient, and the same is true for the unconscious. If I do not engage my rage, it goes on and on; if I do, then I must confront the images it gives of itself. One woman dreamt of herself digging with hands and nails into another woman's neck and shoulders, which was the precise place her fibromyalgia attacked her. Then she consciously engaged the disruptive power of her rage and did not act it out on her body by displacing it into fibromyalgia. The physical pain is real in its own right, but investing rage into it augments it to unbearable intensity.

If we consciously enter the back-and-forth with the unconscious image or body symptom to make clear to ourselves the point of view of this opposing side,[8] as well as the one we endorse, this process of exchange transmutes into a conversation of the greatest value. We meet live parts of ourselves that claim equal attention and will not just go away. We must make room for them, and that changes our whole orientation.

Decades of experience as an analyst have brought home to me the fact that when people consciously experience this transcendent function in themselves, it impresses them as a living something that transcends their ego control and comprehension. As Jung puts it, it feels like the "Unknown as it intimately touches us."[9] The transcendent function slowly moves our ego out of our assumption that we are in charge of our interior life, and builds up a bigger center he calls the Self.[10] Hence, we can often feel the beginning of this process as a disease, a disorientation,

8. See Ulanov, "The Embodied Self," chap. 7, *Spiritual Aspects of Clinical Work* (Einsiedeln, Switzerland: Daimon, 2004); see also Ulanov, *Attacked by Poison Ivy: A Psychological Understanding* (York Beach, Maine: Nicolas-Hays, 2001).

9. Jung, "The Transcendent Function," in *The Structure and Dynamics of the Psyche*, vol. 8 of *The Collected Works of C. G. Jung*, trans. R. F. C. Hull (New York: Pantheon, 1916/1960), p. 68.

10. Ulanov, *Spiritual Aspects of Clinical Work*, chap. 13.

a muddle, and this is another reason we fear it. We suffer! Yet we also feel something new coming on the scene, a new image or even symbol, a breakthrough of feeling, a perception that brings peace. This new thing is not a product of our will or thought, but is "in accord with the deepest foundation of the personality, as well as its wholeness."[11]

This arrival of the new feels like a gift, even grace. I believe it is a main way we feel God operating in us, and Jung says something similar, in that it "possesses compelling authority not unjustly characterized as the voice of God."[12] Through this process we register what Jung means by Self — a bigger center to the whole psyche — and what I mean by Self — a bridge to reality that transcends the whole psyche. We feel as if something looks out for us, what in theological terms we call Providence. It is unmistakably clear to us that we did not produce this new thing, nor did the analyst either. It arrived, its own autonomous, separate, real newness.

God-Images: Subjective and Objective

In thinking about our spiritual journey, this notion of the functioning transcendent helps us in our conversation with our own images for God and the official God-images we receive from our tradition, and with what happens when all these images break down because nothing finite can encompass the infinite free God. We all harbor pictures for God, ones we know about and ones that operate in us unconsciously. A little boy announced "God is Horse," not "the horse" or "a horse" or even "my horse," but "Horse." A woman said that God's heaven to her was like an exciting dinner party full of people of all different races, costumes, and languages, with exotic, regional foods, music, color, all communicating in a great good time — not unlike heaven as a feast, or Christ hosting a wedding banquet. A man dreamt of a cleft-handed God sitting on a low throne with electric energy hissing from his hand when the cleft opened. A woman

11. Jung, "A Psychological View of Conscience," in *Good and Evil in Analytical Psychology,* vol. 10 of *The Collected Works of C. G. Jung,* trans. R. F. C. Hull (New York: Pantheon, 1959/1964), para. 856.

12. Jung, "A Psychological View of Conscience," para. 856.

dreamt of herself with her cross, and Jesus entered it and took her place; then she saw crosses all over, and Jesus entering them and setting people free. We also enjoin group God-images of sisterhood, liberation, evangelical theology, Jungian theory, and our versions of tribal triumph.

Whether individual or group God-images, these are our personal, subjective pictures for God. They are fascinating and as varied as we are from each other. Sunday school or adult religious education gets nowhere unless it finds a way to include these pet gods, these highly personal pictures of the Divine that make it real to us, intimate, speaking to us of our own subjective sense of self.[13]

In addition, unconscious images of God operate in us, ones that act as the center of our existence around which our interior and exterior lives revolve. We could be tyrannized by a problem like an inferiority complex, a drinking problem, an addiction; or our deepest need for money that represents to us security; or the ideal, even a religious ideal to be God's servant — when unconsciously we want to be God's best servant. Such God-images spade up our shadow stuff, which will insist on being included if we struggle to go on praying year after year. The psyche wants to be whole, which does not mean perfect, but that all parts are brought in. God wants all of our heart, soul, mind, and strength, not just the parts we choose. This is coming home, taking acceptance all the way down. The shameful secret, the hidden manipulation, even the murderous intent and, as well, the undared talent and buried tenderness, also get a seat at the table.

These subjective images are gifts from the living psyche. They bring with them consciousness of bits and pieces of self we have lost, parts of us that may be suffering alone in prison, mistreated. One devoutly religious nun dreamt of four women locking a fifth into a dark room. And the woman was blind. The dreamer heard the door click shut upon this woman, and grief filled her heart. Many months later, the dreamer was able to enter into conversation with the locked-up woman, who slowly came out of the dark, entering life again.[14]

13. Ann and Barry Ulanov, *Primary Speech: A Psychology of Prayer* (Louisville: Westminster/John Knox/Press, 1982), chap. 1.

14. For an extended discussion of this example, see Ulanov, *Spiritual Aspects of Clinical Work,* chap. 7, pp. 185-86.

Our religious traditions are chock-full of God-images, and it pays to notice which ones attract us and become our own. We might call these objective God-images; they come to us from Scripture, worship, doctrines, and religious education. They show us aspects of God that we do not know from our own experience; they expose to us the rich and varied treasures in our religious tradition. They break open upon us the words and deeds of the Divine, and God is never separable from word and deed. Hence these images or symbols impart to us the gift of divine presence. Examples include God as rock, refuge, citadel, as fashion designer when Yahweh makes the ephod for the priest, or as tailor when Yahweh sews coverings for Adam and Eve, or as architect designing the temple at Jerusalem. The Psalms sing of God's great wings under which we crawl, of God's thick darkness or unending light, of mysterious presence hovering over the Mercy Seat in the Holy of Holies. In the New Testament, God knocks at our door; appears as landlord, as dinner-party host, as healer, feeder, calmer of the waves, as despised one.

To notice and enter into conversation with these images spurs on our spiritual journey, for this is one way God speaks to us — indeed, knocks on our door. Often a personal God-image may differ greatly from the one to which we adhere in our tradition. Conflict opens up, and we fear it.

Here the shadow material I spoke of in the second essay often appears. What do we do if our compelling subjective image for God challenges our accepted traditional God-image? What if God appears as feminine? Can we just reject that? No. We must engage with that image, for at the very least it brings a part of us into the conversation with God. Maybe I reject parts of the feminine in me, whether I am a man or a woman. Maybe I am oppressed by the discrimination against the feminine in tradition and society. This lost sheep comes on its own to be found, and Jesus goes to fetch it.

Part of our praying and conversing with God will involve our burning personal questions. Theologies in the last thirty years bring such questions into religious discourse. What does God say to me, a person of color, a person politically oppressed, a person of this particular sexual stance, a person physically handicapped, a person mentally ill? How does my context relate to God, and how does God relate to me through this context?

You might object that this has nothing to do with God. But it does, I would answer. This is our stable where God gets born, in this lowly, bodily form, this flesh of day-to-day experience. Through this odd, idiosyncratic image, God comes to find us, bring us home. Our subjective God-images say a lot about us, what shadow parts we need to admit into consciousness. These God-images bring us missing parts of our selves and help us fill out the limited, finite persons we are called to be. It is dangerous to deny these subjective God-images. We refuse the One knocking at our door, saying we want another One, a better One, not the poor Jew from Nazareth. Without including these subjective God-images in our spiritual journey, we can fall victim to a religion of words that do not incarnate. Instead of the living Word, blowing in as the mysterious Spirit, we get empty exhortations and become windbags, or theological know-it-alls, full of what should be, rejecting what is.

An opposite danger results from our falling into unconscious identification with our God-images, whether subjective, objective, personal, or group. We can be overtaken entirely because religious images come from the deepest places in us. They enlist primordial energies that sweep upward from impersonal archetypal patterns and the reality beyond them. All this energy whooshes through our small psyches, our small groups, and we, like corks on the sea, are in the grip of energies not our own. How else do we understand ordinary mortals willing to fly planes full of innocent people, including children, into a building of office workers, bringing death to everyone, and believing they do this in the name of a living God? How else do we understand the group behind them celebrating this as a wonderful fulfillment of duty to the Divine?

Whenever we identify our God-image with God, we become fanatical and theological bullies, trying to force others to agree with us on pain of death. One way I think of Jung's God-image is as consciousness in conversation with the opposite, the unconscious. His identification with that theory got him into trouble. As president of the German psychoanalytical group and editor of its journal, he tried to get Jews and Nazis in Germany to submit articles and thus engage in a back-

and-forth communication that might advance an eventual reconciliation. But this was at a time when even to say you were Jewish could get you killed.[15]

Spiritual journey takes us into hard work. We are asked at once to become increasingly aware, to identify our God-images, both for ourselves and for our groups, and both conscious images and those operating in us unconsciously. These images bring life; they bring us information about ourselves. They are a primary speech of the living psyche and speak both from us and to us, identifying what brings the Holy to us and what we learn about our selves from the Holy. One woman dreamt the question "Where does the Spirit come into you?" The woman asking answered that, for her, it came in from the back. Such images tell us things we need to know about ourselves, shadow materials, broken edges, leaving spaces where God can get in.

It is astonishing to learn that what we thought we believed in, and sincerely do consciously, gets matched by an unconscious God-image that acts as if it is God, in the sense that all of us centers on it. It is our Isaac that we are asked to sacrifice to God, to put God first. Hence our most vexing problem, which consciously we wish to be rid of, may unconsciously act as a little god around which everything else revolves. This problem vies for first place with our conscious God-image. We are asked to sacrifice our inferiority complex to the living God.

Or, it can be the other way around. Unconsciously we dream of an awesome God-image, sometimes joyous, sometimes fearsome. Our conscious religion must come into conversation with this unconscious God-picture because it too belongs. For example, a serious woman, sincere, pious, dreamt of Fred Astaire dancing with joy. He yelled out, "Where is God?" She yelled back, "In your feet!" The dream implies, "Get some life into your faith, some quick step, the gladness of it." A man who consciously believed in the Johannine God of love dreamt that he was bowing down with reverence and fear before a numinous giant pig. This unconscious object does not replace his conscious image of worship, but it cannot be ignored, either. The gap between the two images seems great indeed. But

15. Ulanov, "The Double Cross: Scapegoating," in *Spirit in Jung,* chap. 3.

that is where the work must be done. What is "pig" to him? What is its meaning in the history of symbology? What has it represented as an animal form of deity? The pig represented the mother goddess, so what does he think about maternity, the awesome power of reproduction? This will lead him to explore whatever issues face him, from associations with having children, to overvaluing motherhood, to envy of female power, to the awesome power of nature and his relation to it.

In addition to exploring our God-images, spiritual practice means conversing back and forth in the gap between official God-images — those in Scripture, for example — and our subjective individual and group images. For instance, what goes on in the Exodus story that corrects our making use of it to describe our own emancipation process from racism, sexism, or family prejudice? What in the doctrine of the Trinity instructs our praying so that we realize we have prayed only to one of the three persons, as if one part was the whole three? Just as our subjective images which make God real to us feed the grand traditional images, so those objective God-images offer a dialogue partner, bring us a symbol of the otherness of God as experienced in community through the ages. Our limits meet the vast resources of the community. The rough edges of our idiosyncratic, even neurotic God-images can be rubbed right in exchange with images fashioned by the historic church community. And our too straight, too smooth, too correct God-images can be liberated, opened, jazzed by the odd God-images of the mothers and fathers of the church. We can be sure to find a near neighbor in the worshipping community of two millennia.

For example, we could pair Jung's vision of the green Christ (Jung awoke one night and saw Christ on the cross, "his body . . . made of greenish gold") with Lady Julian of Norwich's vision of Christ's wound at the crucifixion: "I saw the body bleeding copiously . . . in the scourging. . . . The fair skin was deeply broken into the tender flesh through the vicious blows delivered all over the lovely body. The hot blood ran so plentifully that neither skin nor wounds could be seen, but everything seemed to be blood."[16] Jung's keeping the Turin Shroud's face of Jesus

---

16. Jung, *Memories, Dreams, Reflections,* p. 210; and Julian of Norwich, *Showings,* trans. Edmund Colledge, O.S.A., and James Walsh, S.J. (New York: Paulist Press, 1978), p. 199.

hanging covered in his study can be likened to Pascal's hiding in his doublet next to his heart a copy of his overwhelming experience of Christ.[17] The space between subjective and objective God-images, personal and official ones, offers a wide, safe home for the vigorous conversation so necessary to spiritual growth.

Even more demanding is the work set before us by the question, What of evil images or false images? What then? Are we to reject these pictures? Can we never escape them, as poor souls haunted by a punitive, judging God sadly illustrate? In efforts to flee from the scornful, angry voice, it gets exported into punishing violence toward others, with the violent one saying, "God told me to do it." Sometimes the evil image is removed by a traditional God-image. A man in analysis years ago suffered from father-rejection and self-rejection for not being the ideal athlete his parent so desired. The son suffered from retracted toes, curled in on themselves, that made any athletic performance out of the question. Our tracing all this in analysis helped, but the release came through a God-image he beheld on a sabbatical trip to Italy: a mosaic of Christ as Pantocrator in the apse above the altar in a church on the island of Tortcello. There was Christ as eternal, Lord and Judge, with the orb of the world beneath his bare feet, around which his toes curled like talons. These were toes just like this man's! This image freed him to see that the whole person, not toes, constituted the defining aspect. If such toes were good enough for Christ, he need not worry about his own anymore.[18]

These examples do not let us off from responding to the tense question of evil images, false ones. Here decades of clinical work cannot but exert their influence on my reply. All images are true if they are ours; that is the wide-openness of the psyche, giving us a picture of where we are and where we may be led. Mad or distorted images also reveal that that may be where a lost bit of true Self may be hiding. If we scorn the image and say it is unclean, we are moralizing instead of extending a hand to this orphaned bit of ourselves. We shut the door instead of opening it to

17. Jung, *Letters,* 2 vols., ed. Gerhard Adler and Aniela Jaffé, trans. R. F. C. Hull (Princeton: Princeton University Press, 1973), vol. 1, November, 24, 1952, p. 94n.

18. For an extended discussion of this example, see Ulanov, *Finding Space,* pp. 31-32.

this part that would come in and find a resting place, this part that is wandering like the holy couple looking for a place to bring God into the world on Christmas night.

Frightening images need our acknowledgment, not our identifying with them and being carried away, or our rejecting them. They do not go away; they just go unconscious and then present the danger of our projecting them onto our neighbor, into our politics, and onto our jobs. Consciousness provides a container, a testing of reality, and a place to suffer the working out of what these images mean, a suffering that does not have to be inflicted onto our body as illness or onto our children so that they carry the illness for us. Conversation with these images may bring terrific suffering, but it is a suffering that assembles meaning. Unconscious suffering that brings no meaning is worse.

Disidentification and Breakdown

Images for God bring us left-out bits of Self and usher us toward the nearness of the ineffable God to whom they point. We need to identify for ourselves, and our groups, what images operate in and among us. But our journey does not end here, for we use up these images. They are finite, mere pointers. Their very success wears them out. We get to the end of involvement with our God-images. It is as if the images that once helped us know how we know God now lead us into unknowing. We reach the end of the shore, and look out to the vast sea; the end of the light, and peer into darkness; the end of sound, and now hear only silence.

Those of us who have struggled to pray a long time know this ending place, where we disidentify with our images for God and feel close-mouthedness instead. Karl Rahner applauds our arrival: "Whoever does not love the mystery, does not know God; he continuously looks past the true and proper God, and worships not Him but the images of Him made to our specifications."[19]

---

19. Rahner, *Schriften VII*, p. 505, cited in Aniela Jaffé, *Was C. G. Jung a Mystic?* (Einsiedeln, Switzerland: Daimon, 1989), p. 62.

A theological reversal happens at this point: Our questions change. No longer do we ask, "Who are you, God, in relation to me, to us, to my cause of seeking justice in the world, or my panic that my loved child is dying, or my beseeching for answers to my mental anguish?" Now we ask, "Who are you, God? Not as I want you, not as I need you, not as I fear you, but as You? Not of gender, not of color, not of my denomination or theology, not of political or psychological force, but You?" Here we are thrown back into our worshipping tradition, into our Scripture to search again to see, hear, touch, and taste who God has said God is. Once again we feel the full force of the gap between our searchings and constructions for God and who God is — the God who comes across that gap to us in what we might call God's self-image, in Jesus Christ. Here God walks toward us in person, and in Spirit blowing up from we know not where, burning out of our hearts all of our preconceptions. Now we see our God-images as just that — images only, not the it, the that, the suchness, the One who comes. We still have the images, or new ones, but they sit loosely, always with that space between them and what they symbolize.

Another way this disidentification happens comes from the blows of reality. Suffering — in body, in mind, in soul — evicts us from comfortable God-images. Loss, broken relationships, hunger, pain, cruel treatment by other people, poverty, lack of beauty, stupidity — any and all of these introduce into our consciousness the gap between our pictures for God and what God may be. God is not what we wish or need; God is silent; God feels absent. Jesus felt this gap in the Gethsemane garden, praying to the God he knew as his intimate Father, Abba, to whom all things are possible, praying that he need not drink this cup of suffering. Silence answered; abandonment by his closest disciples answered; darkness answered. In this bleak place, Jesus did not know if evil had triumphed and destroyed him, or if evil was gathered up into the providence of God to be defeated by unbroken love. Even Jesus, as human as us, at least in Mark's Gospel, could not get to God from our human side. Resurrection came from God's side, crossing the gap, revealing that the destruction of death did not totally destroy. Love abides, steadfast, bounteous.

Nonetheless, this gap brings danger. Our pictures of God are destroyed, or we rip them up in our great disappointment that God did not make a better plan, so that our beloved need not die. Our objective God-images from Scripture do not bring God near. We sit in the dark. We may panic and turn back, trying to resuscitate our old way of believing. If we succeed, our faith now becomes rigid; we fear questions lest the whole edifice collapse; we deny the gap between God and God-images. Or, we may lose our faith entirely, out of despair at having lost it. We say it never existed in the first place; it was an illusion. We feel paralyzed and cannot get down to the water where the Spirit rustles the surface. Any conversations, connections, or bridges we had break, and we fall into dark unknowingness.

People speak of this plunge as falling into the hands of the living God. We may stay in the dark for decades, taking courage from Teresa of Ávila, who says she prayed twenty-two years before an answer came, or from Julian of Norwich, who said it took her fifteen years to understand her vision of Christ. What happens in this dark that is also a burning light, this consuming fire that burns away all the old starting points, radically cutting into and supplanting what we have known, is the digging up of ground for something new to grow, a different departure point in the making.

Yet we do not know this; we dwell in unknowing. Whatever crosses the gap must come from the other side; we cannot get to God from our side. Yet here is the wondrous fact. We do not need to, for God crosses the gap to us; and we receive (or refuse). Here is the living God, not a dead God held up by repetition in a compulsion to keep religion in place, done by rote, unable to breathe with the breath of Spirit, but a living God. An animating Spirit comes, enlivening us who take the seed and digest it within our living psyche, body, community, politics, history, and day-to-day life. This is creative repetition, like the round of liturgy that marks off space and time, like the round dance pairing with the Eucharist, the dance of joy, the circulation of the living God all through the human family so that we transform into the mystical body of Christ.[20]

20. Jung, "Transformation Symbolism in the Mass," in *Psychology and Religion: West and East*, vol. 11 of *The Collected Works of C. G. Jung*, para. 418.

Presence

What comes across that gap is not words; not a new health plan; not an ethical program or political position paper; not even a new image, nor even a person. For Jesus is dead, killed by our destructiveness, yet not destroyed. What comes across the gap between God and all our finite constructions for God is a living God. And of course we are driven again to use words and pictures to stammer out what comes, such as the famous words of Revelation: "He who sits upon the throne will shelter them with his presence. They shall hunger no more, neither thirst anymore; the sun shall not strike them, nor any scorching heat. For the Lamb in the midst of the throne shall be their shepherd, and he will guide them to springs of living water; and God will wipe away every tear from their eyes" (Rev. 7:15-17).

In psychological language, our subjective pictures for God that mirror back to us parts of ourselves to be gathered into conversation with the sacred — and our objective God-images that declare the treasures culled from centuries of people working over what they receive from God — these both give way to God as objective subject, living, there, external to all our human constructions, free, other; yet here, come to us. We are given new livingness although our language is defeated, our symbols are broken, and our theories that would map this Holy Presence are rendered mere scribbles in the sand. All the human ways that mediated the utterly free God fall into the gap as partial, a ladder we have ascended and of which we now reach the end. We enter unmediated Presence that gives itself to us.

There is no suitable language for mystical experience. Wittgenstein forcibly makes the same point in proposition 6.54 of his *Tractatus Logico-Philosophicus:* "My propositions are elucidatory in this way: he who understands me finally recognizes them as senseless, when he has climbed out through them, on them, over them. (He must, so to speak, throw away the ladder after he has climbed up on it.) He must surmount these propositions: then he sees the world rightly."[21]

---

21. Wittgenstein, cited in Barry Ulanov, "Mysticism and Negative Presence," in *Cre-*

We cannot capture the utterly free God in any of our categories of thought or imagination. This is the genius of Pseudo-Dionysius with his apophatic theology. And it is to be found in twentieth-century deconstructionism too: all our knowledge is relativized by our location, the context in which we know — our gender, class, historical and cultural time, race, creed, and so on. Theology, itself a symbol system, points to what exceeds our grasp that we persist in trying to grasp. Drawing on the mystics' notion of negative presence, Barry Ulanov makes the point that this is not "mere negation or transformation from a lower to a higher plane. It is not the conversion of, say, sexual energy from the flesh to the spirit that is accomplished, but rather the spiritualization of the flesh which for the first time permits the flesh . . . to be itself wholly and truly." This is flesh in the particular, the boundedness of the human body life, cut loose from "class ties" or "categorical essence . . . in the ritual of inspiriting which is mystical experience; it is entirely present; it has presence."[22] We feel the concreteness of divine-human presence as if the world is a limited whole, which is what Jung means by integration. Ulanov likens it to "a fire that descends from the heavens [which] consumes everything by its total identification of a thing, by its radical particularity, by its presenting . . . [us] with nothing less than the *Ding an sich*. . . . And like all burnt offerings of this sort, it gives glory to God."[23]

We are rescued, then, from the tyranny of a person or a group or a religion claiming that they alone know the true God in their fervent devotion and therefore have the right to impose their belief on everyone else. Faith is not exclusive; it is particular. To be concrete and particular, it must be embodied. Hence our way of knowing shifts toward the feminine mode of being: we know in and through daily writing; relating in mind, heart, and strength; not abstracting to construct an intellectual map, such as our official, objective God-images, or retiring into our experience, such as our subjective God-images. God breaks that subject-object dualism and stands forth as objective subject present to us.

ative Dissent: Psychoanalysis in Evolution, ed. Alan Roland, Barry Ulanov, and Claude Barbre (Westport, Conn.: Praeger, 1973/2003), p. 257.

22. Ulanov, "Mysticism and Negative Presence," p. 264.

23. Ulanov, "Mysticism and Negative Presence," p. 264.

A shift occurs from our former task in religious dialogue — to seek intellectual reconciliation of our differing religious experiences — to incarnation. We experience truth touching us in our living. To be received, symbols must be taken into the body, as if eaten, or inseminated, as we join Mary in housing the Holy. This touches Jung's statement that God "is a psychic fact of immediate experience."[24] Our knowing shifts from knowing about to knowing as aligning, as being one with, yet able to speak of it while all the time knowing our words and pictures fall short.

On a smaller scale, in the clinical venture of analysis, this aligning is not unlike the moment in a session when a breakthrough occurs that changes what was and changes what we thought should be. Did it come from the analysand? Did it come from the analyst? It appears to come from between them as a third source that includes both but is not reducible to either. Such experiences, whether religious and/or clinical, prompt a seeing into how to respond to suffering shadow elements in ourselves and in our world. It is in this space where Etty Hillesum, for example, aligns with the joy of life while simultaneously strapping to her back the portion of common suffering afflicting the Jews. She says she guards God's place within her, to which she retreats like a nun withdrawing into prayer, to re-emerge refreshed, to put herself again at the disposal of others in the deportation camp. This alignment mirrors the Son, who dwells in the Father who shows forth in the Son. In Meister Eckhart's vision, in our uncreatedness at the center of our being, we remain with the Son within the Father — a space where God is safe, and we live from the source.[25]

On a larger scale, knowing as alignment hints at the direction to find our meeting of each other in our religious differences: we all look to the same origin point. We meet there in looking to the unoriginated, free origin point. From there our separate incarnations into concrete embodied living show radical particularity, but not exclusiveness, so that we need not endlessly war between your good and my good, which is the problem

---

24. Jung, "Spirit and Life," in *The Structure and Dynamics of the Psyche,* para. 625.

25. For discussion of this point, I am indebted to students in my course called "Psychology of Spiritual Life" (PS 327) at Union Theological Seminary, Program of Psychiatry and Religion, fall semester 2003.

of the twenty-first century. Just as we inhabit different bodies and share the same kind of humanness across our vast differences, so we may see that we share the same origin point and the same kind of task to incarnate its living presence.

Epilogue

On Reading Ulanov:
Scaffolding as Integration

"Integration" is the word the scholarly evangelical community uses to describe so prosaically the conversation between one's faith tradition and the academic disciplines and which Ann Ulanov illustrates so poignantly.[1] In a genuine conversation each partner is open to the insights of the other, allowing the other the right to speak freely and disagree vigorously. Ann Ulanov reminds us that each dialogue partner maintains a separate identity, while at the same time being changed by the interaction.[2] She characterizes herself as standing parallel between psychology and theology and between the ego and the Self. In both cases she encourages conversation. Such a conversation, at best, avoids slighting one tradition — whether by spiritualizing, psychologizing, or biologizing — in favor of another that is esteemed as older or more basic. Integration is hardly like the development of a universal language such as Esperanto, in which the unique identity of languages is sacrificed.[3] Ann Ulanov's objective is not to make Christianity acceptable to

1. Al Dueck, "Integration and Christian Scholarship," in *Integrating Psychology and Theology: Research and Reflections,* ed. Al Dueck (Pasadena, Calif.: Fuller Seminary Press, 2006), pp. ix-xxviii.

2. Ulanov, *Spiritual Aspects of Clinical Work* (Einsiedeln, Switzerland: Daimon, 2004), p. 41.

3. Al Dueck, "Babel, Shibboleths, Esperanto, and Pentecost: Can We Talk?" *Journal of Psychology and Christianity* 21 (2002): 72-80; and Al Dueck, *Between Athens and Jerusalem:*

Jungian perspectives, and she does not simply portray Jung as Christian to make him acceptable to evangelicals. Depth psychology, on the one hand, is a corrective to an overly spiritualized faith, pointing to the everydayness, the messiness of experience and incarnation. Christian theology, on the other hand, has its own voice(s) and may, at some critical points, differ from Jung.

In this epilogue, I wish to honor Professor Ulanov for her dedication to articulating a theological anthropology that utilizes the insights of Carl Gustav Jung. Her dialogue with Jung over the past forty years provides a model for Christian psychologists to emulate. In the three essays published here, she speaks directly to the way Christians can live their lives within the Christian tradition while utilizing Jung's insights along the way.

Over the years, reading books integrating Jung and Christianity, I have often been left with either a Jungianized Christianity or a fully baptized Jung. Some have offered models for how one can converse with Jung: John A. Sanford, Christopher Rex Bryant, Morton T. Kelsey, and Robert A. Johnson.[4] Unlike Ulanov, some of these authors give the impression that Christianity illustrates Jung's notions, or that Christ was a proto-Jungian. There is often little critique of Jung from the perspective

---

Ethical Perspectives on Culture, Religion, and Psychotherapy (Grand Rapids: Baker Books, 1995), chap. 8.

4. See Sanford, *Dreams: God's Forgotten Language* (Philadelphia: Lippincott, 1968); and *The Kingdom Within: A Study of the Inner Meaning of Jesus' Sayings* (Philadelphia: Lippincott, 1970); see Bryant, *Depth Psychology and Religious Belief* (Mirfield, Eng.: Mirfield Publications, 1972); and *Individuation and Salvation* (London: Guild of Pastoral Psychology, 1984); see Kelsey, *Christianity as Psychology: The Healing Power of the Christian Message* (Minneapolis: Augsburg, 1986); *Christo-Psychology* (New York: Crossroad, 1982); and *Healing and Christianity: A Classic Study* (Minneapolis: Augsburg, 1995); and see Johnson, *He: Understanding Masculine Psychology: Based on the Legend of Parsifal and His Search for the Grail Using Jungian Psychological Concepts* (New York: Perennial Library, 1977); *She: Understanding Feminine Psychology: An Interpretation Based on the Myth of Amor and Psyche and Using Jungian Psychological Concepts* (New York: Harper & Row, 1977); *We: Understanding the Psychology of Romantic Love* (San Francisco: Harper & Row, 1983); *Ecstasy: Understanding the Psychology of Joy* (New York and London: Harper & Row, 1989); and *The Fisher King and the Handless Maiden: Understanding the Wounded Feeling Function in Masculine and Feminine Psychology* (San Francisco: HarperSanFrancisco, 1995).

of historic Christian theology. On occasion, Christianity is smoothed, assimilated, even relocated in "the depths" to justify for Christian psychologists the inclusion of Jung's approach to therapy.

Conversation with an academic discipline from a theological perspective is somewhat akin to intercultural or interreligious dialogue.[5] When two very different cultures or religions engage in conversation, an important issue is each partner's point of departure in the conversation. Does one speak in some common dialect or in one's mother tongue? Diana Eck has suggested that in conversations involving various religious traditions, inevitably each person speaks from a particular social and religious location.[6]

Ulanov's confessional foundation is the historic Christian faith. Where Jung departs from that tradition, Ulanov disagrees with him and draws a different blueprint from his. When Jung offers categories that she can use, Ulanov borrows them and/or fills them with Christian content. In a book written with her late husband, a book consistently appreciated by my students, Ulanov uses Jung's insights to enrich the Christian practice of prayer, with an emphasis on the role of desire, the place of imagination, and the importance of vulnerability.[7] Jung, then, functions as the scaffold that aids construction — but he is not the edifice.

The uniqueness of Ulanov's theological conversation with Jung is evidenced in several areas. First, I will examine her response to Jung's perspective on God as subjective experience and/or as independent reality. That, in turn, raises the second issue, that of God's self-revelation in Christ. What is Jung's view of Jesus' role in the life of the individual? Third, I will explore Ulanov's response to Jung's perspective on evil. Jung held strong convictions on the nature of evil and its presence within an individual. Finally, I will move to the relationship of the Self to others in the formation of identity, which I see as another critical point on which

---

5. Dueck, "Babel, Shibboleths, Esperanto, and Pentecost."

6. Eck, *Banaras: City of Light* (New York: Columbia University Press, 1999); and *Encountering God: A Spiritual Journey from Bozeman to Banaras* (Boston: Beacon Press, 2003).

7. Ann and Barry Ulanov, *Primary Speech: A Psychology of Prayer* (Atlanta: John Knox, 1982).

to compare Jung and Ulanov. In each case, I will explain Jung's position as background, raise some general issues, and then bring Ulanov's unique contribution to the foreground.

God

As is already evident in the prologue and in Ulanov's essays, Jung took seriously the experiential encounter with transcendence within the psyche. He felt that any encounter with the Divine, the not-I, had serious psychological consequences. This meeting with the Other rises out of the unconscious and assaults the ego:

> Whoever has suffered once from an intrusion of the unconscious has at least a scar if not an open wound. His wholeness, as he understood it, the wholeness of his ego personality, has been badly damaged, for it became obvious he was not alone; something which he did not control was in the same house with him, and that is of course wounding to the pride of the ego personality, a fatal blow to his own monarchy.[8]

However, a perennial issue is whether Jung viewed God as a reality independent of the psyche. In a 1959 interview on the BBC program "Face to Face," John Freeman asked Jung whether he believed in God. Jung's answer was, "I do not need to believe in God; I know."[9] Jung claimed he remained silent with regard to the objective nature and existence of God. His focus, he said, was psychological, on the inner impact of the Divine on the human psyche. He hoped to avoid both the dogmatic and the metaphysical. Jung commented, "Any statement about the transcendent shall be avoided, for such a statement is always only a ridiculous presumption of the human mind which is unconscious of its boundaries."[10] On the

8. Jung, *Nietzsche's Zarathustra: Notes of the Seminar Given in 1934-1939*, vols. 1 and 2, ed. J. L. Jarrett (London: Routledge, 1989), vol. 2, p. 1233.
9. An audio clip of this excerpt is available on the Web site of the Jung Society of Atlanta: http://www.jungatlanta.com.
10. Richard Wilhelm and C. G. Jung, *The Secret of the Golden Flower: A Chinese Book of Life* (New York: Harcourt, Brace & World, 1931), p. 135.

other hand, Jung wrote in a letter to P. W. Martin, "The main interest of my work is with the approach to the numinous . . . but the fact is that the numinous is the real therapy."[11] Three days before he died, Jung said, "To this day God is the name by which I designate all things which cross my willful path violently and recklessly, all things which upset my subjective views, plans and intentions."[12] These comments leave one confused about whether or not Jung acknowledged God beyond the psyche.

If indeed Jung was incapable of confessing a God independent of the psyche, then the archetypes housed in the collective unconscious become *ipso facto* the surrogate god-term: the archetype is neither learned nor acquired through culture, and its meaning is similar across cultures. Based on the ubiquity of the cultural themes he noticed in his self-analysis and in the psychotic patients he saw at the Bürgholzi Hospital, Jung proposed that the form of the archetypes was universal, while culture filled in the content. Human life is dependent on the archetypes. Like most god-terms, these primordial forms (unknowable) and images (the products) are assumed to give life meaning. The powerful effect of these images is a consequence of their autonomy; like the gods, they just show up. "In this image certain features, the archetypes or dominants, have crystallized out in the course of time," Jung explained. "They are the ruling powers."[13] While Descartes had proposed that reason was common to humanity, Jung thought that the archetypal structures provided a common foundation. Though his archetypes have precursors in Plato's Original Ideas, the archetypes are Jung's form of foundationalism. The archetypes, like divinity, order human life; they enable self-regulation. In the absence of an objective God, the subjective archetypes serve a god-like role.

On the other hand, if the numinous is an identity independent of the psyche, what can be said about the God who stands behind the arche-

11. Jung, letter to P. W. Martin, 20 August 1945, quoted in Andrew Samuels, *Jung and the Post-Jungians* (London: Routledge & Kegan Paul, 1985), p. 16.

12. Jung, cited in Edward Edinger, *Ego and Archetype* (Baltimore: Penguin Books, 1972), p. 101.

13. Jung, *Collected Works*, vol. 7, para. 151, quoted in Samuels, *Jung and the Post-Jungians*, p. 27.

typal images that emerge in the soul and limit the ego? Does this God invite a person into a relationship in which human character is ethically transformed? Emmanuel Levinas, noted Jewish philosopher of the past century, has reminded us of the importance of alterity, or otherness.[14] He has emphasized the ethical demand that the Other places on us to love and not to harm. Even more radically, Levinas believes that the Other assaults the ego, interrupts the flow of consciousness with obligation and does so not from within the psyche but from beyond. He is less concerned with ontological union with the Divine and more concerned with the God whose mystery is beyond our thematizing.[15]

If the numinous appears through an archetype, how can the numinous relativize the ego in Jung's system? Using the insights of Levinas, Lucy Huskinson points out that there can never be a complete definition of the Self. If the Self is defined as a whole, as total, as the unification of the opposites, then the Self is simply a *necessary* postulate in a closed psychological system. Then God is truly not Other.[16]

How does Ulanov respond to Jung on this issue? In these essays, Ulanov builds on the Jung who abhorred reducing God to the Self.[17] As a theologian, Ulanov affirms the God who exists independent of the psyche. In her first essay, she states unequivocally, "More than three decades of clinical work have brought me to the clarity that the Self, in Jung's jargon, is not God, but is that within us that knows about God."[18] Note in the following quotation how she moves beyond pure subjectivity:

> In dealing with our projections in the area of religious value we need to become consciously related to the God-within, the psychic image

14. Levinas, *Totality and Infinity: An Essay on Exteriority* (Pittsburgh: Duquesne University Press, 1969); and *Otherwise Than Being: Or, Beyond Essence* (Boston: M. Nijhoff, 1981).

15. Levinas, "Ethics of the Infinite," in *Debates in Continental Philosophy: Conversations with Contemporary Thinkers,* ed. Richard Kearney (New York: Fordham, 2004), pp. 65-84.

16. See Huskinson, "The Self as Violent Other: The Problem of Defining the Self," *Journal of Analytical Psychology* 47 (2002): 437-58.

17. See especially the first essay in this volume.

18. See the first essay in this volume, pp. 33-34.

we project onto God in Jung's language, the archetype of the self — and also consciously to relate to the God-without. We must deal with what traditional systems of value tell us about God in order to gain access to our subjective experience of the Divine, to gain access to the God of which organized religions speak.[19]

To fail to make this distinction between the inner and the outer opens us to the charge of idolatry.[20] Ulanov's affirmation is critical for the construction of a model of the person that is appropriate for Christians.

What are the characteristics of this God? Ulanov understands God as the one who comes to us in the person of Jesus Christ. She states,

> God has come and entered our long day's dying, our being dust, and to dust we return; God has taken up into God's self the suffering that human life entails, which we magnify by inflicting it upon each other. God has taken responsibility for creating us free creatures who can refuse God, taking the consequences onto the cross, where the innocent Holy One suffers as if guilty. The logic of evil stops here.[21]

Ulanov uses Jung as a scaffold in her work with clients. She agrees with Jung that how one experiences God is refracted in the structure of individual personality. Men might experience God differently from women, introverts from extroverts, scientists from artists, ancients from moderns. In a psychologically sensitive culture, few would disagree that the patterns that have built up in the psyche over time filter whatever images of God the individual might experience.[22] Those aspects that are split off, rejected, or overshadowed need the light of day in order to be addressed.

Ulanov views her work with clients as occurring in the presence of God. Together they circle around God as center, avoiding the danger of idolatry or solipsism. She says that "what we are doing together is circling around the same center, a surround that holds both our egos and

19. Ulanov, "The Self as Other," in *Carl Jung and Christian Spirituality,* ed. Robert L. Moore (New York: Paulist Press, 1988), p. 57.

20. Ulanov, "The Self as Other," p. 58.

21. See this volume, p. 62.

22. J. B. Phillips, *Your God Is Too Small* (New York: Macmillan, 1953).

simultaneously dissolves their ascendancy."[23] She quotes Rilke: "I am circling around God, around the ancient tower, and I have been circling for a thousand years, and I still don't know if I am a falcon, or a storm, or a great song."[24] We dialogue with God as we listen to the client's narrative of pain in a three-way conversation. The critical issue becomes not pathology, but how close we are to this Center. This understanding radically equalizes the power difference between therapist and client. Neither the client nor the therapist can depend solely on other people.

Jung is clear about the danger of hubris in the identifying of the ego with the Divine. However, he is less clear about Who the stimulus is for God-images appearing in the soul. Ulanov sees the importance of heeding the transcendent images arising in the soul, and she affirms those images when they are consistent with the Christian tradition. Evangelicals need a structure to stabilize the soul while it is deconstructed in repentance and reconstructed in transformation, as God builds a temple of wholeness.

Christ

Is God experienced only internally, shrouded in mystery, or is God experienced also in concrete form? How would one recognize this inner force as beneficent or malevolent? In the Christian tradition, we discover in the person of Jesus Christ the nature of Yahweh, the "I will be who I will be" (Exod. 3:14).

In various places in the corpus of his writings, Jung addresses the meaning of Jesus' life for the individual and for society. Jesus in fact is so psychologically significant for Jung that he appears in Jung's dreams:

> One night I awoke and saw, bathed in bright light at the foot of my bed, the figure of Christ on the Cross. It was not quite life-size, but extremely distinct, and I saw that his body was made of greenish gold.

23. Ulanov, *Spiritual Aspects of Clinical Work*, p. 23.

24. Ulanov, *Spiritual Aspects of Clinical Work*, p. 23. See R. M. Rilke, *Selected Poems of Rainer Maria Rilke,* trans. Robert Bly (New York: Harper & Row, 1981), p. 13.

The vision was marvelously beautiful. And yet I was profoundly shaken by it.[25]

Jung grants that Jesus was a significant historical figure, a "wandering miracle Rabbi," an archetypal person.[26] We should imitate him, Jung suggests, but in the sense of living "our own proper lives as truly as he lived his in its individual uniqueness."[27] For Jung, this is not simply a matter of *imitatio Christi,* the imitation of Christ, because he believes we must each take up our own cross of suffering, be caught between our personal contradictories, and move toward greater individual consciousness. An over-identification with Jesus as the perfect figure could result in an underestimation of the power of the shadow in the life of the believer.[28] Because Jesus withstood the temptations in the wilderness, Jung felt that Jesus had cut off the shadow side of his personality. Hence, Jung tells us, we are *not* to imitate Christ by following his example.

Jesus does exemplify for Jung the archetype of the Self,[29] and Jung suggested that Christ remains the critical symbol for the West. His life follows the archetype of the hero common in the folklore of various cultures. Says Jung,

> The most important of the symbolical statements about Christ are those which reveal the attributes of the hero's life: improbable origin, divine father, hazardous birth, rescue in the nick of time, precocious development, conquest of the mother and of death, miraculous deeds, a tragic, early end, symbolically significant manner of death, postmortem effects (reappearances, signs and marvels, etc.).[30]

25. Jung, *Memories, Dreams, Reflections,* trans Richard and Clara Winston (New York: Vintage Books, 1961), p. 210.

26. Jung, *Letters,* 2 vols., ed. G. Adler and A. Jaffé, trans. R. F. C. Hull (Princeton: Princeton University Press, 1975), 2: 205.

27. Jung, *Psychology and Religion: West and East,* vol. 11 of *The Collected Works of C. G. Jung,* trans. R. F. C. Hull (New York: Pantheon, 1938/1958), para. 340.

28. Jung, *Aion: Researches into the Phenomenology of the Self,* vol. 9b of *The Collected Works of C. G. Jung,* trans. R. F. C. Hull (Princeton: Princeton University Press, 1959), para. 245.

29. Jung, *Aion,* p. 37.

30. Jung, "A Psychological Approach to the Dogma of the Trinity," in *Psychology and*

The stages that Christ passed through are the stages we must all go through.[31] Jesus is the form of the God-man as evident in the Self, the goal of wholeness. In the West, the God-image, which lives in everyone, is best seen in Christ. More important than the objective, historical Jesus is the Jesus within, seeking incarnation in our lives. However, for Jung, "the Christ-symbol lacks wholeness in the modern psychological sense since it does not include the dark side of things but specifically excludes it in the form of a Luciferian opponent."[32]

Kant proposed that the two categories of space and time were inherent in reason and ordered our perception of the world. Speaking of Jesus, Kant foreshadows Jung:

> In the appearance of the God-Man (on earth), it is not that in him which strikes the sense and can be known through experience, but rather the archetype, lying in our reason, that we attribute to him (since, so far as his example can be known, he is found to conform thereto), which is really the object of saving faith, and such a faith does not differ from the principle of a course of life well-pleasing to God.[33]

Just as Kant rescues reason from Humean skeptics with his epistemological archetypes of space and time, Jung salvages the numinous — as archetypes found in the collective unconscious — from modern religious skeptics.

If Jesus' significance is archetypal, is the Jesus of the Christian Scriptures the norm for what it means to be human?[34] Does one test the messages of the collective unconscious, of dreams and intuitions, with the call to be followers of Jesus in life and death? Would these archetypal im-

---

Western Religion, trans. R. F. C. Hull (1948; Princeton: Princeton University Press, 1984), pp. 50-51.

31. Edward F. Edinger, *The Christian Archetype: A Jungian Commentary on the Life of Christ* (Toronto: Inner City Books, 1987).

32. Jung, *Aion,* p. 41.

33. Kant, *Religion Within the Limits of Reason Alone* (New York: Harper Torchbooks, 1960), pp. 109-10. I am indebted to Brian Becker for drawing this to my attention.

34. G. Clarke Chapman, "Jung and Christology," *Journal of Psychology and Theology* 25 (1997): 414-26.

ages ever suggest kenosis, self-emptying? Phillip Rieff notes that in sacral cultures, revelation is the source of ethics and the delineation of human nature.[35] However, since Jung's Christology is not constructed on the historic Christian confession, the content and meaning of the Christ archetype is filled in inductively from various cultural motifs, the archetypes.

Jung claims that he is speaking of the experience of the psyche and not speaking dogmatically, though it is not always clear whether he maintains that distinction.[36] Ulanov is more careful in distinguishing between orthodox beliefs and subjective experience:

> Christian tradition talks about this concretization as the Incarnation. One cannot receive or participate in God's truth *in abstracto;* one can only hear it through the words and presence of the person of Jesus and of the reactions of countless persons to him throughout history. Only through the human does the divine make itself known.[37]

Ulanov affirms the Chalcedonian creed when she says,

> Here is a picture of a God who enters into human suffering, who in Christ takes on himself the agonies, sorrows, and griefs of humans overcome by sin and captured by the principalities and powers of evil. What the Son suffers, the Father suffers, for they are of the same substance.[38]

Furthermore, Jesus is the God we can touch and who touches us in our bodies and our dreams.[39] Ulanov states in her first essay that "experience of the theological fact of Jesus Christ comes to us through the psy-

35. Rieff, *My Life among the Deathworks: Illustrations of the Aesthetics of Authority* (Charlottesville: University of Virginia Press, 2006).

36. For example, Jung states after describing Jesus as unitemporal and eternal, unique and universal, that "this formula expresses not only the psychological self but also the dogmatic figure of Christ. . . . The parallel I have drawn here between Christ and the self is not to be taken as anything more than a psychological one. . . ." See Jung, *Aion,* pp. 63, 67.

37. Ulanov, "The Self as Other," p. 60 (italics in original).

38. See this volume, p. 65.

39. Ulanov, *Spirit in Jung* (Einsiedeln, Switzerland: Daimon, 1990/2005).

che, as does all experience."[40] However, she also speaks of God's self-disclosure in the humanity of Christ:

> Here we are thrown back into our worshipping tradition, into our Scripture to search again to see, hear, touch, and taste who God has said God is. Once again we feel the full force of the gap between our searchings and constructions for God and who God is — the God who comes across that gap to us in what we might call God's self-image, in Jesus Christ.[41]

Ulanov sees the contribution of depth psychology as prophylactic; it grounds spirituality in matter, in the body, and prevents it from becoming wholly ethereal. Hence, spirituality must address issues of aggression, sexuality, and interpersonal hurts in everyday life in order to avoid being an "airy-fairy thing, without tonus, without tissue aliveness, without guts."[42] We need a spirituality, she suggests, that requires both the conscious ego, though deposed, and the current of the unconscious.

So, while Jung makes Christ into an idealist archetype and at the same time emphasizes the importance of a grounded spirituality, Ulanov sees in Christ a model of groundedness, the incarnation of the character of God. This will require the hard work of interpreting how Christ is construed within, so that the God in Christ is more clearly reflected. For evangelicals, Jung's subjectivity faces a critical test in the nature of the Incarnation. Is Jesus fully and solely one of us, showing us the way in our search for God in a unique way?

Evil

In contrast to a psychology shorn of morality, which rejects the language of good and evil as quaint moralism, Jung's approach is a profound reminder of something that Christian psychologists have known but may

40. See this volume, pp. 39-40.
41. See this volume, p. 84.
42. Ulanov, *Spiritual Aspects of Clinical Work*, p. 16.

have forgotten given the hegemony of modernist psychological discourse. More than any other psychotherapist, Jung recognized the presence of evil in human life — and specifically in the lives of his clients. He urged his clients to confront not only the shadows in their souls but also, and even more, the evil that lurked there. Moral language is not foreign to a Jungian perspective.

Jung criticized Christians for not taking seriously enough the dark side of humanity. They spoke abstractly about fallenness and human depravity, Jung thought, but they often avoided wrestling with the subjective reality of the shadow elements of the psyche. Although the shadow is not necessarily equated with evil in parts of oneself, there remains a tendency to deny embarrassing personal elements. Furthermore, more serious than failing to identify the dark aspects within oneself is the proclivity, according to Jung, to fail to recognize the negative side of God, which Jung found especially present in the Old Testament.[43]

How is it possible for Jung to speak with such confidence about the nature of evil in the modern world, with its kaleidoscope of moral and ethical communities? Therapy as a moral enterprise requires an ethical context that provides at least a minimal consensus on what behaviors are ethically inappropriate. Just as Jung confidently labels as positive certain images arising from the collective unconscious, he also assumes that negative symbols will emerge. This raises the question of how the images come to be perceived as positive or negative, good or evil. Jung's approach to ethics is autonomous rather than heteronomous; he does not depend on an external, received ethical tradition to interpret behavior as good or evil. Don Browning has argued for the critical role of a moral context for healing.[44] Similarly, Alasdair MacIntyre has maintained that a tradition is necessary to interpret moral terms, that there is little moral consensus about the meaning of such terms in the modern

43. Jung, *Answer to Job,* trans. R. F. C. Hull (London: Routledge & Kegan Paul, 1954); and John Thurman, "In the Shadow of the Almighty: A Jungian Interpretation of Negative God Images in the Pentateuch," Ph.D. thesis, Fuller Theological Seminary, School of Psychology, 2003.

44. Browning, *The Moral Context of Pastoral Care* (Philadelphia: Westminster Press, 1976).

world, and that all we have left are fragments of earlier approaches to justifying moral judgment, whether utilitarian or deontological.[45]

Ulanov begins with confessionally derived convictions regarding what is bad.[46] She suggests that as we work through issues in therapy, we encounter the effects of the Fall. While Jung projected evil into the God-head, Ulanov takes a different approach — placing the conflict with evil squarely within the psyche. She comments that for Jung, "evil and good are principles of being itself, constantly in strife. All archetypes are bivalent. It is at the archetypal level that Jung's good-and-bad God dwells."[47] Our images of God are mixed, Ulanov says; both good and evil are present. This is the struggle of the Self.

In response to Jung's emphasis on evil, Ulanov unflinchingly points out Jung's inconsistency in colluding with the Nazis. Jung later admitted to postwar leader Leo Baeck, "I slipped up."[48] During his editorship of the *Journal of the International General Medical Society for Psychotherapy*, Jung, in Hegelian fashion, assumed that by publishing the opposing views of Jewish and Nazi doctors, something new would emerge. As Chair of the Analytical Society, Jung, along with his colleagues in the group, placed a cap on the number of Jews who were allowed to be members. Jung was also a member of the Analytical Psychology Club of Zurich. The discovery in 1989 of a secret appendix to the organization's 1916 by-laws,[49] which limited Jewish membership to 30 percent, has given rise to considerable criticism.[50] Ulanov sees Jung's involvement in such policies as one of his blind spots. She states,

---

45. MacIntyre, *After Virtue: A Study in Moral Theory* (Notre Dame: University of Notre Dame Press, 1984); and *Whose Justice? Which Rationality?* (Notre Dame: University of Notre Dame Press, 1988).

46. See the second essay in this volume.

47. See this volume, p. 61.

48. Quoted in Aniela Jaffé, "C. G. Jung and National Socialism," in *From the Life and Work of Jung,* trans. R. F. C. Hull (New York: Harper, 1971), pp. 97-98.

49. Richard Noll, *The Jung Cult: Origins of a Charismatic Movement* (Princeton: Princeton University Press, 1994), pp. 259-60.

50. However, it should not be forgotten that three of Jung's closest colleagues were Jewish: Erich Neumann, Jolande Jacobi, and Aniela Jaffé.

Jung is singular among depth psychologists in his intense interest in evil, in taking up good and evil as moral categories, in probing the mystery of conscience. Yet Jung did not recognize one of the greatest examples of evil in history when it confronted him in its immeasurable brutality.[51]

Jung, who placed such importance on the integration of the opposites, failed to understand that some opposites are integrated at our own peril. Again Ulanov says,

> In the *privatio boni,* evil is indeed understood to exist, but in a very different way from good. Good is simply being in relation to God, related being, created being, being within the circle of dependent connections to the Creator. Evil denies that connection, seeks to destroy it, to defect from it. Evil exists as denial, betrayal, deficiency, a ruthless attempt to put "nothing" in the place of something. Evil exists outside relation to a transcendent center, usurping the center for its own version and vision of reality. Isn't this exactly what the Nazis attempted?[52]

The incorporation of evil did not increase consciousness. Consciousness, Ulanov points out, betrayed Jung. "Consciousness of the opposites and writing about them in categories of Aryan and Jew, of the Germanic and the Jewish, harmed instead of helped, brought attack instead of a healing clarity."[53] Ulanov suggests that instead of integrating the opposites, one should intercede on behalf of the shadow and the Self within. Evangelicals need Jung's call to recognize evil. Too often, they have codified evil into proscribed acts and then closed their eyes to its relational, social, and political reality. Jung suffered from similar blindness.

---

51. Ulanov, *Religion and the Spiritual in Carl Jung,* p. 52.
52. Ulanov, *Religion and the Spiritual in Carl Jung,* p. 52.
53. Ulanov, *Religion and the Spiritual in Carl Jung,* p. 53.

Self and Other

A repeated criticism of Jung concerns his failure to articulate a perspective of relationality to match his finely tuned delineation of the individual psyche: ego, Self, shadow, persona, personal and collective unconscious, anima and animus, introversion and extroversion. In the opening of *Memories, Dreams, Reflections*, Jung states, "Thus it is that I have now undertaken, in my eighty-third year, to tell my personal myth. I can only make direct statements, only 'tell stories.' Whether or not the stories are 'true' is not the problem. The only question is whether what I tell is my fable, my truth."[54]

Communal religious traditions hear the voice of God in Scripture, tradition, and personal experience. In the author's Anabaptist tradition, spirituality is social in nature, and immersion in the life of the Christian community is critical to spiritual formation. The Christian as part of the church is a witness to the larger society. The church is called to speak with authority as it seeks to interpret the meaning of Scriptures for daily life. It is a community of accountability,[55] and spirituality is not simply a personal matter.[56]

While Ulanov is most appreciative of Jung's view of the subjective self, she stresses to a much greater extent the importance of human sociality. Ulanov relativizes experience by tradition. For her, tradition is alive with images, rituals, and symbols. Tradition expands the ego beyond the narrow confines of its own obsessive needs to include the other. Ulanov is not content with analysis that simply ends with greater awareness of unconscious processes. Analysis must move on to a consideration of the human other. "Only through relation to others, then, can one have any notion of self at all, and only through concrete personal relationships can one draw

---

54. Jung, *Memories, Dreams, Reflections*, p. 3.

55. See Donald Kraybill, *The Upside-Down Kingdom* (Scottdale, Pa.: Herald Press, 2003); John Roth, *Beliefs: Mennonite Faith and Practice* (Scottdale, Pa.: Herald Press, 2005); and John Howard Yoder, *Body Politics: Five Practices of the Christian Community before the Watching World* (Scottdale, Pa.: Herald Press, 2001).

56. See David W. Augsburger, *Dissident Discipleship: A Spirituality of Self-Surrender, Love of God, and Love of Neighbor* (Grand Rapids: Brazos Press, 2006).

near to the sense of value in abstract objective dimensions."[57] While Ulanov is sensitive to the inner life, her view is global. She states, "Self has to do with the whole of reality, both within and without, and with the ages, the human story under the light of eternity."[58]

Ulanov's more social perspective is apparent also in her affirmation of specific traditions. She is a particularist in that she identifies with the Christian tradition, and it shapes her reading of Jung. Indeed, she has commented, "Faith is not exclusive; it is particular."[59] To be concrete and particular, it must be embodied. Ulanov states,

> The ways we conduct our spiritual journey, and the ways it conducts us into greater intimacy with God, operate in the space between the subjective images we have for God and the objective ones we receive from our religious tradition, and in the space between all our human images for the Holy and the Holy itself, which breaks every image because nothing we construct can harness the infinitely free God. . . . We feed the traditions of dogma by making them real through our idiosyncratic images of God; tradition feeds us by bringing to us what countless minds and prayers have turned over and refined, which exceeds what our limited perceptions can achieve.[60]

Jung seeks renewal from within the individual, and the price he pays is that he slights the relational. Ulanov corrects that weakness with her sensitivity to interpersonal and global issues.

Conclusion

The gift of Ann Ulanov is apparent in the way she models a nuanced conversation between herself as a theologian and Jung as a psychologist. The tone of the conversation is neither strident nor polemical, but gracious and individuated. Ulanov warns that our shadow may include becoming

57. Ulanov, "The Self as Other," p. 39.

58. See this volume, p. 34.

59. Ulanov, in a statement made in response to a question at the symposium held in Pasadena, California, 2004.

60. See this volume, pp. 70, 71.

overly identified with our psychological theory;[61] thus her response to Jung varies with the issue at hand. Sometimes Ulanov clearly and critically disagrees with Jung. At other times she sets forth a constructive critique of his inconsistency and uses Jung in ways that are consistent with her theological convictions. She avoids the extremes of uncritical acceptance or wholesale rejection of Jung's views. She does not "make him" Christian but asserts that his views are helpful to the religiously sensitive therapist.

Ulanov uses Jung's work as scaffolding to assist her work as a person of faith. In this response to her dialogue with Jung, I've examined four areas that support this assessment. In her response to Jung's view of God, Ulanov's style of integration involves differing with Jung theologically, but taking seriously the psychological impact and centrality of God's presence in healing. She unhesitatingly affirms God as independent of the psyche, yet she encourages exploration of subjective God-images. For those Christian psychologists eager to be "professional" as defined by a secular guild, Ulanov sounds a warning and sets an example: The human psyche is religious in nature and experiences God subjectively, and this is psychologically relevant in therapy.

Ulanov's Christology reflects Jung's emphasis on embodiedness; but she fills that concept with the Incarnation, the body of Christ. For Ulanov, ethical normativity emerges less from the numinosity of the archetypes and more from the example of Christ's life. At the same time, she affirms the archetypal material that bubbles up from the collective unconscious and indicates how Christ is culturally and personally experienced in the human psyche.

In her analysis of evil, Ulanov illustrates most clearly her ability to discern the similarities and differences between herself and Jung. Ulanov takes note of Jung's ideas about the presence of evil but holds him to his psychological perspective — there can be no projection of evil onto a non-subjective God. Ulanov avoids idealizing Jung. Graciously and courageously, she points out his failings in regard to the Jewish community. She refuses to psychologize evil, and she stresses the presence of evil in the individual, in society, and in culture.

61. See the second essay in this volume.

Finally, though Jung leans toward affirming the individual, Ulanov affirms both the individual and tradition. In her many books, she freely uses the Jungian model of the psyche — but qualifies it with an emphasis on community. We are left not with one more paean of praise for the modern individual, but with a call to greater personal integrity and social responsibility.

Ulanov's message to therapists is clear: To take spirituality seriously means that we address it in our own lives *and* look for it in the lives of our clients. Like Jung, she unabashedly views religion as integral to an understanding of the person and also to healing. She reminds us of the depth of the human soul, in contrast to the shallow psychology often appropriated by the church.[62]

I conclude with Ulanov's encouragement to therapists in *Religion and the Spiritual in Carl Jung:*

> This religious dimension must be recognized one way or another. It wants to penetrate concrete life, achieve some visible form. This means that in training mental health professionals to help people who are mentally distressed or emotionally disturbed, the training must take account of one's own religious life or non-religious life, one's own God-images, one's own complexes around religion. If we fail to do this, this unexamined religious life will adversely affect our countertransference reactions as easily as do unexamined sexual complexes, images, or drives. In training, we must do the hard reading in spiritual and religious texts that we do in psychological texts to construct a bigger territory to draw upon in our work. It also means we must make the spiritual dimension a part of the whole treatment. It is not something tacked onto the end of treatment like a pretty scarf to embellish a psychological outfit we have worked hard to put together.[63]

ALVIN DUECK

---

62. See E. Brooks Holifield, *A History of Pastoral Care in America: From Salvation to Self-Realization* (Nashville: Abingdon Press, 1983).

63. Ulanov, *Religion and the Spiritual in Carl Jung,* p. 44.

CPSIA information can be obtained
at www.ICGtesting.com
Printed in the USA
LVHW042302190623
750169LV00031B/287

9 780802 824677